PowerPoint Magic

Pamela Lewis

Includes CD with
Lesson Templates and
Assessment Resources

International Society for Technology in Education
EUGENE, OREGON • WASHINGTON, DC

PowerPoint Magic

Pamela Lewis

Director of Book Publishing
Courtney Burkholder

Acquisitions Editor
Jeff V. Bolkan

Production Editor
Lynda Gansel

Production Coordinator
Maddelyn High

Graphic Designer, Book Design and Production
Signe Landin

Book Sales and Marketing Manager
Max Keele

Developmental Editor
Michael van Mantgem

Copy Editor
Mary Snyder

Cover Design
Kim McGovern

Library of Congress Cataloging-in-Publication Data

Lewis, Pamela, 1956-
  PowerPoint magic / Pamela Lewis. — 1st ed.
     p. cm.
  ISBN 978-1-56484-235-0 (pbk.)
  1. Education, Elementary — Computer-assisted instruction. 2. Middle school education — Computer-assisted instruction. 3. Microsoft PowerPoint (Computer file)   I. Title.
  LB1028.5.L4965 2008
  371.33'4558—dc22

                                                                    2008003117

First Edition
ISBN: 978-1-56484-235-0

Printed in the United States of America

International Society for Technology in Education (ISTE)
Washington, DC Office:
       1710 Rhode Island Ave., NW, Suite 900, Washington, DC 20036-3132
Eugene, OR Office:
       175 West Broadway, Suite 300, Eugene, OR 97401-3003
Order Desk: 1.800.336.5191
Order Fax: 1.541.302.3778
Customer Service: orders@iste.org
Book Publishing: books@iste.org
Rights and Permissions: permissions@iste.org
Web site: www.iste.org

About ISTE

The International Society for Technology in Education (ISTE) is the trusted source for professional development, knowledge generation, advocacy, and leadership for innovation. A nonprofit membership association, ISTE provides leadership and service to improve teaching, learning, and school leadership by advancing the effective use of technology in PK–12 and teacher education.

Home of the National Educational Technology Standards (NETS), the Center for Applied Research in Educational Technology (CARET), and the National Educational Computing Conference (NECC), ISTE represents more than 85,000 professionals worldwide. We support our members with information, networking opportunities, and guidance as they face the challenge of transforming education. To find out more about these and other ISTE initiatives, visit our Web site at **www.iste.org**.

As part of our mission, ISTE Book Publishing works with experienced educators to develop and produce practical resources for classroom teachers, teacher educators, and technology leaders. Every manuscript we select for publication is carefully peer-reviewed and professionally edited. We look for content that emphasizes the effective use of technology where it can make a difference—increasing the productivity of teachers and administrators; helping students with unique learning styles, abilities, or backgrounds; collecting and using data for decision making at the school and district levels; and creating dynamic, project-based learning environments that engage 21st-century learners. We value your feedback on this book and other ISTE products. E-mail us at **books@iste.org**.

About the Author

Pamela Lewis graduated from the University of Witwatersrand with a B.A. degree in education. After teaching French, English, history, and mathematics, she completed a bachelor's degree in psychology at the University of South Africa. Lewis was appointed to the French subject committee in the province of Transvaal, designing curriculum and developing study guides for teachers. After immigrating to the United States, she worked as a part-time French teacher in Milwaukee, Wisconsin. During this time she completed an M.S. degree in computers in education at Cardinal Stritch University.

She currently works as a technology training and documentation coordinator at Marquette University in Milwaukee, Wisconsin. Lewis has taught computer classes to students in kindergarten through eighth grade and worked with teachers to integrate technology in the curriculum. She also works part-time as a technology consultant, and has trained teachers in the Archdiocese of Milwaukee Schools and other school districts, doing some work for the Stephens Group. She has taught graduate classes for the Outreach Program of St. Mary's University of Minnesota and for Cardinal Stritch University.

Other ISTE books by Pamela Lewis

Spreadsheet Magic, 2nd Ed.

Contents

Introduction

PowerPoint is an effective and engaging tool for communication, visualization, and graphic representation. But it is PowerPoint's special features that make it the tool of choice for elementary and middle school students. Students love to use the software: it engages their attention, and the visual tools stimulate creativity. They can easily master the technical skills required to produce professional-looking documents with pictures, backgrounds, animation, and interactivity. This book helps teachers provide young writers with a way to express their ideas and to be effective writers and communicators.

As teachers, we can use PowerPoint to foster visual learning and to develop critical thinking skills. Visual tools change the nature of writing, providing students with color, fonts, clip art, and photographs that work together with the verbal components of communication. As a result, young writers are able to enhance their message. They can organize their writing in a nonlinear format using hierarchical structure to compose and to have main ideas and details visible simultaneously. Students might structure their ideas, for example, by inserting a diagram, organizational chart, or table.

The lessons provided in *PowerPoint Magic* describe how first-grade through eighth-grade students can use this tool for writing, visualization, and graphic representation. Templates are provided for most lessons. Younger students use templates that contain some pre-created formatting and graphics so students can focus on the learning objectives without needing to master the software. Templates further help younger students by including step-by-step instructions on the slides or in the Notes pane. Relevant Internet links are given, providing a wealth of resources for young learners.

This book illustrates how, through using PowerPoint, students can become active producers rather than passive consumers of multimedia. In the exercises offered in this book, students are able to select, organize, and integrate verbal and pictorial material to make sense of information and build understanding and knowledge. I encourage educators to embrace this powerful tool for learning.

A Powerful Tool for Learning

PowerPoint has many special features. In the following pages, we'll explore why these features make PowerPoint a valuable tool for younger students.

PowerPoint is one of the most commonly used applications (Keller, 2003), being used by more than 75 percent of schools (Hlynka, et al, 1998). Used by both teachers and students, the PowerPoint application is often already installed as part of the Microsoft Office Suite on most school computers. But even given its widespread use, myths about PowerPoint abound.

Let's take a look at some of the myths about PowerPoint and along the way explore its potential in student writing, communication, and learning.

Myths about the Educational Usefulness of PowerPoint

Myth 1: PowerPoint software is used only for making slide shows and for giving oral presentations that often lack substantive, organized content. These types of presentations are ineffective when students focus on multimedia effects. Transitions, animations, sounds, color, images, and hyperlinks become distractions, and these tools hinder rather than enhance meaning and communication.

PowerPoint Magic demonstrates how teachers and students can use PowerPoint to write and present for an audience. Although this multimedia authoring program allows the user to add sounds and videoclips, the lessons in this book focus on learning, writing, and communicating by emphasizing thoughtfully arranged text and graphics in a variety of compelling ways. PowerPoint is much more than just a presentation tool.

Myth 2: PowerPoint limits creativity by providing boilerplate templates for students to use.

This book demonstrates how young writers can create slides from scratch or make use of creative templates designed by the classroom teacher.

Myth 3: PowerPoint requires information to be presented in bulleted lists.

You'll discover in *PowerPoint Magic* that students do not need to use bullets just because the slide layout automatically places a bullet on the slide. Indeed, many writing formats and options are available in PowerPoint.

Myth 4: Early elementary students cannot use PowerPoint independently.

The magic of PowerPoint is that it allows teachers to adapt the use of the templates for mastery-appropriate levels. Young students are able to use the software if some of the tasks have been done for them. They master new skills one at a time and soon become proficient at using the program. Even first-grade students can move easily from slide to slide, enter text, and insert and move clip art.

PowerPoint applications can motivate students of all ages to learn and create. PowerPoint offers students access to an array of visuals to help them organize and interpret concepts and information. It is the role of the teacher to structure PowerPoint assignments so that students are able to write, communicate, and learn with increasing confidence. The teacher meets the challenge by guiding the students' engagement and creativity.

PowerPoint as a Desktop Publishing Tool

Edward Tufte (1998) discusses "visual information design" and suggests that seeing intensifies thinking and that graphic design helps conveys ideas. When students present written words with colors and graphics, the visuals add voice to the words in the same way that oral inflections can change the way listeners interpret the meaning of words. Students can become engaged on more levels as they incorporate multimedia options into their writing.

Clip art: Myriad images are accessible in PowerPoint's Clip Art Gallery. If this component is not available, your tech support personnel can help you enable access to that resource. Microsoft Office Online's Clip Art and Media Home, accessible from within the program, also increases the size of the library of accessible clips. The search feature encourages students to work carefully. For example, to find a specific picture they will need to use correct spelling when they enter words into the search bar.

Drawing tools: Students learn basic composition lessons when they use drawing tools to group and ungroup pictures, selectively delete parts of a picture, or change line color and fill color. They can also rotate and layer pictures in order, and send them behind or in front of text. Then, using text boxes, callouts, or speech bubbles, words can be added to pictures to express an idea. The results can be story illustrations, advertisements, and shape poems (Fig. 1).

Figure 1. This shape poem was made by a student using drawing tools and WordArt.

Fonts and Backgrounds: Using PowerPoint, students convey nuances of meaning by manipulating the appearance of words. They design a product by formatting fonts, font color, size, and style. They may choose to align text to the left, center, or right; they may change the spacing, highlight important headings, or use bullet points to itemize a list. WordArt adds options in terms of text orientation and shape, pre-designed colors, and styles.

PowerPoint users can choose a background color and pattern or apply a ready-made background. They can apply the background to all slides or change the background for one particular slide.

Photographs: PowerPoint makes it is easy to insert pictures taken with a digital camera. Using the Picture tool, students are able to crop, lighten, darken, and increase contrast of photographs.

In some of the lessons in *PowerPoint Magic*, students pose for photographs, take their own photos, and insert photos into slides. Role-playing and dressing as an adult helps spark students' imaginations, and using PowerPoint helps prompt them to reflect on, effectively consolidate, and expressively communicate their learning experiences.

Moreover, in conjunction with PowerPoint, students can use a drawing program such as Microsoft Paint (one of the free accessories on a PC) to further modify their photographs to dramatize and interpret a scene from a reading assignment (Fig. 2).

Figure 2. Students demonstrate creativity as they manipulate photographs to distort reality and help communicate their understanding of a fantasy novel.

Layout: PowerPoint gives students an opportunity to determine how to use the white space on a page or slide, and to decide where to place text boxes, clip art, photographs, or drawing objects. They can make guides for layout visible, which helps them decide how to balance white space evenly and to center objects.

Print Options: PowerPoint print options allow students to make booklets or full-size posters. PowerPoint helps students learn to organize their oral presentations using speaker notes that they print on the Notes Pages.

PowerPoint as a Writing Tool

Using PowerPoint, student writers add details to written phrases and sentences. The Title and Text slide layout lends itself to writing a topic sentence and details. Students can make an outline and use keywords to brainstorm ideas. They can use clip art and text boxes to make a visual plan or graphic organizer. The teacher can make templates with writing prompts for students. Photographs and pictures help stimulate ideas for writing.

PowerPoint offers various ways of viewing the hierarchical structure. As shown in Fig. 3, each slide has its main idea in the title and details in the text box.

Figure 3. Title and Text layout for slides gives a structure for writing. The main idea is in the heading and the details are in the text box.

Outline view helps writers remember the big picture as they work on the details of each slide (Fig. 4). Student writers can also switch to Notes view for more details.

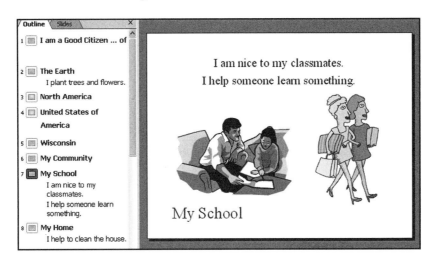

Figure 4. The Outline view remains visible (left) as students brainstorm ideas and add details to each slide (right).

Using these features, students do not need to proceed in linear order and can easily move from slide to slide; the amount of text that can be placed on a slide automatically increases as the font size shrinks. Students accustomed to writing on paper may have to learn how to jump from place to place as they write, leaving draft ideas, and returning to modify or expand their ideas later. The act of writing is often a nonlinear experience, and PowerPoint can assist students in understanding the dynamics of the writing process.

Likewise, students can refer to Internet resources as they brainstorm and develop their ideas. They can resize their windows so that both PowerPoint and the Internet are visible at the same time, making the move between applications easy.

Visual Organization

As students create slides, they organize in both visual and verbal modes. Student writers often improve organization when they use tools that provide multiple views and represent hierarchical idea structures in a visual display.

Normal view: Working in Normal view, students begin with an outline in the Outline pane and then add details to each slide in the Slide pane. They can see the outline and the slide simultaneously. As they get the idea of writing in hierarchical levels, they can use the Increase Indent and Decrease Indent buttons on the Formatting toolbar to promote and demote topics in the Outline pane. They improve the structure of their writing by dragging and dropping as they highlight and move chunks of text.

Sorter view: In Sorter view, ideas can be placed in order (PowerPoint slides are rearranged graphically). Slides can also be duplicated or copied; then the duplicate can be modified.

Notes Page view: While main ideas are placed on slides, details can be arranged or listed in the Notes Page view. In this view, students see the slides and make notes that, for example, could be used during an oral presentation.

Diagrams and Organizational Charts: Diagrams and organizational charts may be inserted in slides (Fig. 5). Several lesson templates provide students with a graphic organizer, Venn diagram, or flow chart to help them organize ideas.

Figure 5. Organization charts can double as graphic organizers to help students better understand a topic of study.

Concept maps include verbal and nonverbal formats, helping to make information easier to remember. Graphic organizers help students to link new knowledge to existing knowledge (Fig. 6). Advanced graphic organizers help students focus on key elements.

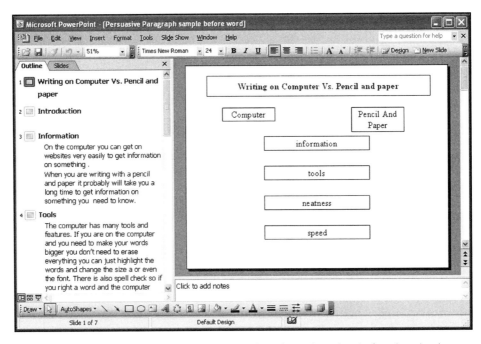

Figure 6. The graphic organizer on slide 1 helps students focus their ideas before they develop those ideas on slides 3 and 4.

Tables: Tables may be inserted, providing a format for students to compare and contrast ideas and organize information.

Animals	One helped One harmed	One helped One not harmed or helped	Both helped
Dog and flea	X		
Sea anemone and clown fish			X
Whale and barnacles		X	
Giraffe and oxpeckers			X
Cleaner shrimp and blueface angelfish			X

Figure 7. Students use this table to compare the symbiotic relationships between animals.

Exporting to a Word Processing Program

Students can begin writing in a PowerPoint document and then export the outline format to a Word document. They then delete headings and change formatting to paragraph style.

Though not demonstrated in this book, it is also possible for young writers to write an outline in Word and export it into a PowerPoint slide show, such that each main idea is presented on its own slide. Pictures and speaker notes can then be added to complete the presentation.

Hyperlinks and Nonlinear Organization

Inserting nonlinear hyperlinks to other slides and to Web sites allows students to produce interactive products with nonlinear structure, constructing a network of interconnected ideas. Students seem fascinated with this new opportunity for arranging ideas.

Grammar, Spelling, and Other Writing Tools

PowerPoint is much more than a presentation software. It also contains some powerful word processing features.

Spell Check: This tool helps students with writing conventions by underlining errors with a red wavy line. Students are quick to learn how to right-click the under-lined word and select the correct spelling from suggestions made by the spelling checker.

Pen Tool: This tool is used to write or draw on a slide. It can be used to monitor and modify sentence fluency. Students take note of writing traits while using the pen tool in Slide Show view, as it clearly shows edits and suggestions (Fig. 8).

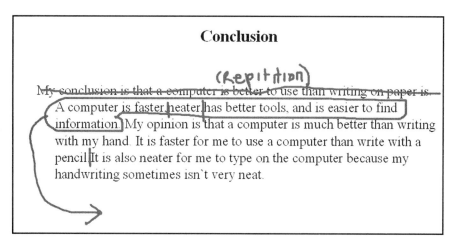

Figure 8. Students edit each other's writing in Slide Show view. The author reviews the peer editor's suggestions and modifies the work before removing all comments.

Word Count: Young writers can use this tool to check the length of sentences, drawing their attention to possible run-on or overly long prose.

Grammar Check: This feature points out grammatical mistakes, including incomplete or run-on sentences.

6+1 Writing Traits

The lessons in this book help student writers develop vocabulary and improve word choice as they read, participate in class discussions, and make posts on online discussion boards. The skills they will need to effectively communicate are highlighted below. Please refer to definitions and scoring guides at the Northwest Regional Educational Library Web site, www.nwrel.org.

1. Ideas

Content or theme

Students use the Internet to explore, research, and develop ideas. Graphics, like clip art, photographs, and videoclips also help them generate and develop ideas.

2. Organization

Structure

Students use editing tools to organize writing, such as Drag and Drop, Cut and Paste, Insert. They use visual cues to organize writing in graphic organizers and use the outline and detail on slides to create a hierarchical structure. They also organize in new ways using nonlinear links to make interactive slide shows or to link to Web Pages.

3. Voice

Personal tone

Engaged learners, who are inspired and motivated, care about the projects they make, present to a real audience, or make a booklet, badge, bookmark, poster that looks professional. Students take great pride in their work.

4. Word Choice

Vocabulary to convey meaning

Students may use an online thesaurus, dictionary, or rhyming dictionary to help with word choice.

5. Sentence Fluency

Sentence structure and rhythm

Attention is drawn to sentence structure when each sentence is placed on a new line after a paragraph is written. It is then easy to identify sentence beginnings to see if they are the same. It is also easy to compare the length of sentences.

6. Conventions

Correct spelling and grammar

Spelling, grammer, and style checkers help writers with conventions.

6+1. Presentation

How the writing looks on the page, includes verbal and visual elements

Original artwork, photographs, fonts, colors, and backgrounds add meaning to words. Students use desktop publishing skills to help communicate a message.

Collaborative Writing

PowerPoint offers students a professional-looking way to share their knowledge, understanding, vision, or story. When they work as a group, they have an opportunity to solve problems with their peers. Students can work on individual slides that can be inserted into a group slide show. This combined slide show can then be printed as a group book or booklet. As students engage in a collective project, the class becomes a learning community with common goals.

Communicating with PowerPoint

PowerPoint is used primarily as a tool for making presentations. When students use it for this purpose, they are encouraged not to write the words they will speak on the slides (and merely read the words to the audience), but to place main ideas on the slides and details in Notes Page view. Students love to create with images, clip art, animation, sounds, and special effects to capture their audience's attention.

PowerPoint is more than just a presentation device. The classroom-tested lessons in this book demonstrate how students use the software to help them communicate with verbal and visual cues as they narrate stories, write descriptions, investigate and research, instruct their peers, persuade others, compose poetry, and visualize problems and concepts by making graphic representations.

Narrative Writing Lessons

Children often identify with the characters of a story. They empathize as characters feel excited, amused, happy, sad, stressed, or relieved. Through storytelling, children explore different ways to behave, the consequences of actions, and how to resolve problems. They also enter the world of fantasy. They learn to make up their own stories.

While writing their narrative in PowerPoint, students have easy access to pictures, and this helps them link verbal and visual images. Beginning writers construct sentences with words that they are learning to spell. The easy use of clip art allows them to illustrate or to represent words they may not yet know how to write.

Young students begin to focus on the ordering of events and story elements as their stories become more complex, as we will see in the My First Stories lesson. Using PowerPoint, they can add, delete, and rearrange ideas and sentences. For them it is magic.

Being able to combine clip art, photographs, and a young writer's own written text often stimulates creativity. In the Halloween Stories lesson second graders dress up as the characters in a class storybook about Halloween and then write using their own photographs for inspiration.

In the Digital Storytelling lesson, students re-read classic children's books and make a picture book for a kindergarten "buddy." As these more mature writers focus on language mechanics, story structure, character development, setting, and plot, they develop an awareness of story presentation in terms of illustrations and font used. More advanced students can make the story interactive by inserting buttons that lead to other slides for more information or a different ending.

In the Visualize, Dramatize, and Retell a Story lesson, students communicate the theme of a chapter using both visual and verbal tools. They select a chapter from a novel or a story they have read. Then they stage an incident, photograph themselves in the role of the characters, write about the meaning of the extract they have chosen, and present their adaptation to the class. These young authors use the tools in PowerPoint to communicate meaning, and focus on creative ways that a story can be retold.

Descriptive Writing Lessons

In the What Do I See? lesson students begin expository writing as they describe photographs that reflect what they discover in an experiment with fruit and seeds. They might also comment on slides that contain photographs inserted by the teacher, or they might write with a pencil on handouts printed three per page with lines for writing.

PowerPoint has an interface that students use for writing and looking at photographs at the same time. In the Guess Who I Am? lesson, first graders use templates with writing prompts that provide a structure for them to introduce themselves to new classmates. The students use pictures, photographs, and words to share information. In the Main Ideas and Details lesson older students learn to structure their descriptive writing by first noting main ideas in the Outline pane and then adding details to the slides.

Research Writing Lessons

Students research a topic and communicate information and knowledge to the reader or audience in the Celebrating our Culture, Penguins, The Year in Review, and Internet Research 101 lessons. In the Celebrating our Culture lesson, students begin by brainstorming what they already know about the subject matter. They are given questions about cultural celebrations, they search for the answers on an online encyclopedia site, and then they use a Venn diagram to compare celebrations across cultures. In the Penguins lesson, elementary students investigate penguins and share their research with classmates. They use multiple information sources for ideas— magazine articles, Web pages, encyclopedias, or a video, for example. They formulate questions and then use research materials to find detailed answers. They report their findings in their own words. As a lesson extension, students then compare penguins to other birds.

In the Year in Review lesson, upper elementary students complete an in-depth exploration of significant events of that year, then pick one current event to research. They use preselected online resources, magazines, and newspapers to search for information. They explain the event and create an outline of why the event was important to them. In an extension to this lesson students investigate a current event online and use Who, What, Where, When, and How to write a lead article as a newspaper reporter. Middle school students structure their investigation using a KWHL table (Fig. 9). They plan their research, explore different ways of accessing information online, and record what they have learned.

What I **K**now	What I **W**ant to learn	**H**ow I will learn	What I **L**earned

Figure 9. KWHL tables help students structure research assignments.

The Big6 Research Technique (see Table 2) provides a structure for dealing with research projects. It helps students break down the process into logical steps.

Older students learn about search techniques in the Internet Research 101 lesson. Because of the ease of copying and pasting pictures and text in the computer environment, young writers need to understand the importance of citing their sources and avoiding plagiarism.

Younger students acknowledge the source of information or pictures by listing just the title of the source, for example, Worldbook Online. A bibliography slide is included with some templates in PowerPoint where the information can be added. Older students include more complete references. They may need guidance about format and are directed to the requirements of the APA or MLA format. Several Web sites offer help in formatting references, including Son of Citation Machine (www.citationmachine.net) and Knight Cite (www.knightcite.com).

As students complete the lessons offered in *PowerPoint Magic*, they gradually develop their investigation skills as they research topics such as bats, penguins, life cycles, heroes, and symbiosis.

Students will explore Internet research strategies and learn the importance of validating sources and using varied techniques. They use the Internet Research template to guide their research path on a given topic (Fig. 10).

Starting point	Keywords/Path	Resource #1	Resource #2
Directory Yahooligans directory www.yahooligans.com	Social studies-history-biographies-authors-Walker, Alice	http://www.galegroup.com/free_resources/bhm/bio/walker_a.htm	http://voices.cla.umn.edu/vg/Bios/entries/walker_alice.html
Ask in plain English Ask for Kids www.askforkids.com	Who is Alice Walker?	http://www.ask.com/web?o=0&qsrc=6&q=Why+Is+Alice+Walker+Famous	http://www.luminarium.org/contemporary/alicew/
Boolean terms (+, "") Alltheweb.com advanced search www.alltheweb.com	AND "Alice Walker" AND author	http://en.wikipedia.org/wiki/Alice_Walker	http://www.we.pdx.edu/alicewalker/walker.html
Metasearch engine Ixquick www.ixquick.com	Alice Walker	http://members.tripod.com/chrisdanielle/alicebio_1.html	http://womenshistory.about.com/library/bio/blbio_walker_alice.htm
Pictures Google Images	Alice Walker	www.speakersworldwide.com	www.womensart.com
Online Encyclopedia www.worldbookonline.com	Alice Walker	http://www.worldbookonline.com/wb/Article?id=ar589880&st=alice%20wal	Alice Walker

Figure 10. Students use this table to direct and record their search for information on a given topic. They note the address of the starting point, the terms they enter to search at this site, and two Web addresses of relevant information found from each starting point.

Table 2. Steps in the Big6 research technique

	Description of this phase of research	Task for the learner
1. Task Definition	Brainstorm ideas and develop thoughts.	Define the problem, and write questions to be answered.
2. Information Seeking Strategies	Use graphic organizers, keywords, symbols, colors, and pictures to make nonlinear connections.	Determine sources of information; evaluate their worth, and how to access the information.
3. Location and Access	Organize main ideas and supporting details on a graphic organizer.	Find the information, by listing keywords and using books and the Internet.
4. Use of Information	Students internalize what they have learned and create an original product written in their own words.	Read the source and take notes on the relevant information.
5. Synthesis	Organize information from multiple sources Using diagrams they have made, students add new information to what they already know. Make an outline.	Make a product to share the learning: a multimedia presentation, oral presentation, or written paper. It must include a bibliography.
6. Evaluation	Identify what students don't know, and show them mistakes in the connections they have made.	Evaluate your own work, and determine how to improve on it.

Instruction Writing Lessons

Many agree that we learn best by teaching. Some of the lessons offered in *PowerPoint Magic* guide older students to teach younger ones about specific content and technology skills. In the Shape Up! lesson older students share their expertise as photographers and mathematicians while helping primary students make shapes booklets. Regardless of a project's complexity, older students should assist their younger buddies, not do the job for them.

In the case of first graders who take photographs and find shapes for themselves, the older buddy inserts the photographs into a PowerPoint slide show for the younger buddy and then the younger students work independently to label the shapes.

Upper elementary students, for example, can explain to younger students about the Presidents of the United Sates, after verifying their facts online. In the Presidents Day lesson, older students use PowerPoint to make an interactive slide show that, on the surface, teaches younger students about the presidents (Fig. 11). Along the way, however, these older students also demonstrate advanced technology skills to their younger peers as they copy, paste, and arrange elements from other programs into the presentation.

Figure 11. This interactive slide show was made by an older student to teach a first grader about presidents. Two possible answers are offered on this slide, and the learner chooses one, which links to a slide saying "Well Done!" or "Try Again!" A back button then returns the learner to this slide so that he or she can continue with the slide show.

Persuasive Writing Lessons

Most of us know that advertisers exploit the impact of visual messages to influence consumers and sell products or ideas. Modeling what they see in the world around them, students can learn to use the tools in PowerPoint to enhance nonverbal communication. In the Buy Me! lesson students review advertisements and analyze words and visual cues to discover how advertisers persuade the public to purchase their products. Students use WordArt to create their own persuasive ad.

In the Persuasive Paragraphs lesson, students discuss a controversial topic with fellow students via an online discussion board. They add topics or conversation threads and respond to others' ideas while using a slide outline in PowerPoint to structure their writing and refine their position. Finally, they document the results and write an essay about the experience in paragraph form.

Poetic Composition Lessons

Poetry is a powerful way to communicate ideas. In the First Rhymes lesson, early elementary students can identify rhymes as they learn their vowel sounds. Using PowerPoint, they make connections between words, sounds, and pictures; they read and illustrate the poems; and they have fun making their own rhymes as they find rhyming words and compose short poems (Fig. 12).

THE CAT AND THE FIDDLE

Hey diddle diddle, the cat and the fiddle,
The cow jumped over the moon,
The little dog laughed to see such sport,
And the dish ran away with the spoon.

Jesse
is messy
and too mean
to clean

Figure 12. Using PowerPoint, students can identify rhymes by changing the font.

In the Mother's Day Poem lesson upper elementary students write a poem with a given structure in terms of number of lines and rhyme scheme. Using a template helps them adhere to the format.

Older students learn to use figurative language in the Picturing Poetry lesson. Using PowerPoint they can make a booklet to show that they understand figures of speech, using pictures to help convey their message. Figure 13 shows a student illustration of a metaphor.

Students use the visual tools in PowerPoint as they write shape poems, in which the words themselves become part of the illustration. Students give a visual structure to their words by composing poems using the diamante or cinquain structure (Fig. 14). They enhance and stimulate their writing by paying attention to the impact of visual communication.

Figure 13. A student illustration of a whispering wind

Figure 14. A sample student diamante poem that was written, formatted, and illustrated using PowerPoint tools.

Visualization and Graphic Representation Lessons

Visual tools offer techniques to enhance learning. Students simultaneously process words and mental images as they match ideas and pictures. PowerPoint's use of pictures helps students to visualize the meaning of difficult or abstract concepts.

In the Greater Than, Less Than, or Equal To? lesson students create and solve math problems using pictures to represent numbers. This helps students connect abstract numbers and mathematical symbols with concrete objects to develop understanding of mathematical concepts. The Simple Machines lesson helps students visualize new concepts through creating a booklet that defines and illustrates each type of simple machine they find.

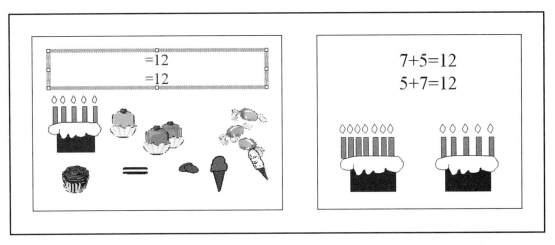

Figure 15. Students reorganize pictures on a template to create visual representations of a math problem.

Richard E. Mayer (2001) presents a theory of "cognitive multimedia learning" that goes beyond verbal learning to build and connect picture-based and word-based representations. The learner mentally creates verbal images and pictorial images, helping them understand, retain, and generalize meaning. His theory suggests that:

1. Students learn better when words or verbal information are combined with pictures or visual information.

2. Cognitive overload occurs when the learner's cognitive processing exceeds his or her cognitive capacity.

3. Deeper learning occurs when the learner is actively engaged, integrating or building connections between words, pictures, and previous knowledge. Active learning is stored in long-term memory, and it can be used to solve transfer problems.

4. Learning with multimedia improves retention and transfer.

Mayer asserts that the learner must engage in the following cognitive processes for meaningful learning to occur:

1. Selecting relevant words

2. Selecting relevant images

3. Organizing selected words

4. Organizing selected images

5. Integrating word-based and image-based representations: Here the learner connects the verbal and the visual and connects with prior knowledge.

Scope and Sequence Chart of PowerPoint Skills

The lessons in this book require a certain amount of basic computer literacy for students and teachers alike, as illustrated in the following table. The asterisk indicates the student may need assistance.

COMPUTER SKILLS	Grade								Teacher
	1	2	3	4	5	6	7	8	
Enter text in a text box	X	X	X	X	X	X	X	X	X
Highlight text; change font, font color, size, and alignment	X	X	X	X	X	X	X	X	X
Use the Undo button on the Standard toolbar	X	X	X	X	X	X	X	X	X
Navigate from slide to slide using the mouse, Page Up, Page Down	X	X	X	X	X	X	X	X	X
Navigate from slide to slide using the scroll bar	X	X	X	X	X	X	X	X	X
Insert pictures from file; move, and resize	X*	X*	X	X	X	X	X	X	X
Insert, move, and delete clip art	X	X	X	X	X	X	X	X	X
Resize and duplicate clip art	X	X	X	X	X	X	X	X	X
Insert clip art from Microsoft Office Online Clip Art	X*	X*	X	X	X	X	X	X	X
Use Print Preview, print a document	X	X	X	X	X	X	X	X	X
Print handouts two, three, or six per page	X*	X*	X*	X*	X*	X*	X	X	X
Take photos with a digital camera	X	X	X	X	X	X	X	X	X
Open a document, Save As		X	X	X	X	X	X	X	X
Insert, size, and move a text box		X	X	X	X	X	X	X	X
Copy a picture from a drawing program (e.g., Kid Pix) and paste it onto a slide		X*	X	X	X	X	X	X	X
Layer or order pictures or drawings		X*	X	X	X	X	X	X	X
Format slide background		X	X	X	X	X	X	X	X
Right-click a hyperlink and open it		X	X	X	X	X	X	X	X
Use the task bar to move between a PowerPoint document and a Web browser		X	X	X	X	X	X	X	X
Copy a picture or text from a Web page and paste it into a PowerPoint document		X	X	X	X	X	X	X	X
Enter information in the Outline pane, details on the slide			X	X	X	X	X	X	X
Use the Increase Font or Decrease Font buttons to change font size			X	X	X	X	X	X	X
Add or remove bullets in text boxes			X	X	X	X	X	X	X
Delete a slide			X	X	X	X	X	X	X
Insert and format WordArt			X	X	X	X	X	X	X
Use the line and arrow tools			X	X	X	X	X	X	X
Select more than one piece of clip art at a time			X	X	X	X	X	X	X

Scope and Sequence Chart of PowerPoint Skills *continued*

COMPUTER SKILLS	1	2	3	4	5	6	7	8	Teacher
Run spelling checker, right-click words that are spelled incorrectly to get help with correct spelling			X	X	X	X	X	X	X
Copy and paste a Web page address				X	X	X	X	X	X
Draw basic shapes				X	X	X	X	X	X
Change the color of shapes				X	X	X	X	X	X
Draw a text box				X	X	X	X	X	X
Group and ungroup drawings				X	X	X	X	X	X
Format fill and color of an object				X	X	X	X	X	X
Format line width				X	X	X	X	X	X
Use Line tools and Autoshapes				X	X	X	X	X	X
Move objects with the mouse or the arrow keys				X	X	X	X	X	X
Hold down the ALT key and move objects without snapping to the grid				X	X	X	X	X	X
Export the words in a slide show to a Microsoft Word document					X	X	X	X	X
Print the slide show in Notes Page view					X	X	X	X	X
Use the zoom function on a digital camera, turn off the flash					X	X	X	X	X
Upload pictures from a camera to a computer, save photos					X	X	X	X	X
Crop photographs, change the brightness					X	X	X	X	X
Rotate a text box or a graphic					X	X	X	X	X
Insert callouts or speech bubbles					X	X	X	X	X
Set the timing on a slide show					X	X	X	X	X
View toolbars					X	X	X	X	X
Move between Normal view and Slide Show view					X	X	X	X	X
Print full-page slides						X	X	X	X
Use Page Setup to change page orientation						X	X	X	X
Set Print area, then print select slides						X	X	X	X
Insert a hyperlink into a file from a Web site						X	X	X	X
Insert action buttons or hyperlinks into a slide,						X	X	X	X
Insert music or voice recordings						X	X	X	X
Animate graphics						X	X	X	X
Copy notes from Web pages, keeping a PowerPoint and a Web browser window open at the same time. Resize windows so that both are visible at the same time.						X	X	X	X
Make notes on a slide in Slide Show view using the pen or highlighter tool						X	X	X	X

Teaching with PowerPoint

The ideas and guidelines in *PowerPoint Magic* have been designed for teachers, principals, curriculum coordinators, technology integration specialists, media specialists, and teacher educators. As a resource for instruction, with lessons designed for classroom teachers across the curriculum, educators can use this book to help students develop and hone their thinking, writing, and technology skills.

How to Implement the Lessons in this Book

The lessons found in *PowerPoint Magic* are designed to appeal to all learning styles. What follows are some things to keep in mind as you implement these lessons to suit your individual needs.

Student Technology Skills

Keyboarding skills are crucial. In my experience with first through eighth graders, most students prefer to do an assignment on the computer. Younger students who have not yet mastered the keyboard may take a little extra time to find the keys, but their skills develop with practice.

In each class there may be a couple of students who get too distracted with the multiple tasks to complete an assignment. I sometimes print out part of the project for students if they get frustrated with slow keyboarding skills; then they complete the rest on the computer at their own pace.

Time Constraints

The amount of time that students have access to the computer is very important, especially for younger students, who take longer at every step.

Give students time limits to complete the tasks, and offer rubrics where content is weighted more heavily than technical accomplishments. Students will be happily engaged if they are given enough time to perfect photographs, pictures they draw and paint, animations, and sound effects, but due to time restrictions, it is better to introduce students to the creative possibilities and then concentrate on the ideas rather than on perfecting the use of the tools. Many students pursue this on their own once their interest has been sparked.

Technical Support

A classroom teacher who supports the use of technology and expects quality work from students can help them produce outstanding work. The teacher may need help from a computer specialist or parent volunteer who has experience or training on computers. In one school, first- and second-grade lessons were conducted with at least two adults present in the computer lab—a technology integration specialist, a classroom teacher, and sometimes a parent volunteer. We have some parent volunteers who have come to us with advanced technology skills, and many parents enjoy learning along with students.

Basic Hardware and Software

Students need access to well-maintained computers with Microsoft PowerPoint (including the Clip Art Gallery component) installed on them. Maintenance problems cause a lot of frustration and discouragement. At our school, we are fortunate to have a laboratory of 30 computer stations that students have access to once or twice per week. Our largest class is smaller than 30, allowing each student to work at their own station or share computers on collaborative projects. Though 1-to-1 computer access for each student is optimal, the author realizes that it is not always possible. Therefore, all of the assignments in this book could be completed in a classroom with one or a few computer stations.

Projector

Many projects may be adapted as large-group activities, making it easy for students to see demonstrations with a video projector or a large screen television. An alternative option is to simply have students gather around a monitor to see the computer screen. Students are able to participate directly and share their knowledge and expertise when they use an interactive white board or SmartBoard. At our school we use a projector in the computer lab to demonstrate skills; we have a white board to write down key words or new vocabulary for students, and a SmartBoard to encourage participation.

Alternative suggestions for the one-computer classroom: Use templates as worksheets, or take turns. Rotate by having one student learn how to accomplish and master the task and then have that student teach a second student while a third student watches how it is done. The second student then teaches student number three while student number four observes. You may want to write keywords and draw tables and charts on your white or black board.

Color Printer

Students who communicate with color will of course need a color printer. Prices for printers are reasonable, although it is still expensive to replace color cartridges. Nevertheless, these costs are not excessive if color is used sparingly. For example, guide students not to print slides with color background. Less ink is used when slides are printed two or six per page.

Shared Network Folders

Computers should be networked to allow students to open files from a shared or general folder. This can be done without a network by using CDs, disks, or other portable storage devices to access and save files, but having a network streamlines the process. Networked computers also allow students to each work on a portion of a project and to combine slides prepared at different stations into one group assignment.

Digital Camera

A digital camera is a powerful, easy-to-use, and affordable tool that engages students (Fig. 16). Photographs can be downloaded to the computer or saved onto CDs, disks, or other portable storage devices, depending on the camera. At one point, my school purchased a set of 10 very cheap digital cameras for students as young as first grade to use. Special offers are available for purchasing cheap basic digital cameras from time to time.

Figure 16. A boy photographs his friends to get a picture of a rectangle to make a Shapes book. They then insert their pictures into a slide show. The picture on the right shows a page from a student's Shapes book showing the circle shape.

Internet Access

Students use pre-selected Web sites in several assignments in this book. They can right-click a link on a PowerPoint slide and then click on Open Link to open a Web browser. It's helpful to create a page of links for younger students. Links can be pasted into a Word document and saved as a Web page, and the browser can be set to open to this as the home page. (Using Internet Explorer, click on the Tools menu, then Internet Options and then paste in the address of the document.) As a result, young students only have to click on a link to get to a specific Web page. Web sites can also be bookmarked or entered as favorites on each individual station. Be sure to include good starting places such as a kid-friendly search engine or a directory like Yahooligans (http://yahooligans.yahoo.com), or an online multimedia encyclopedia. If it is financially possible, it's worth subscribing to an online encyclopedia. World Book (www.worldbookonline.com) provides text and pictures that have been carefully screened for accuracy and age appropriateness. I discourage students from doing their own online research, as it can be a time-consuming and complex task. Upper elementary students need guidance and training. There are assignments in this book to help them develop those skills.

Outline of Lessons in this Book

These lessons are infused with hard-earned, real-world classroom experience. In each assignment, students demonstrate their learning and understanding of critical concepts through the product they create. As they make their slides, they become information producers rather than passive consumers. Constructivism theory states that the learner actively builds knowledge and skills and understanding improves when a learner relates details to the whole. The material in this book is divided into manageable pieces, or meaningful "chunks," or segments, to help facilitate learning. Brain-based learning theories imply that students learn when motivated; the classroom-tested lessons in this book will engage and motivate students.

Lesson Description

Each lesson in *PowerPoint Magic* begins with a description of the lesson. It explains how teachers introduce the topic, building on students' previous knowledge, and how they engage students. The section also describes how the templates on the accompanying CD are used in the lesson.

Assessment

This section offers resources (rubrics and checklists) that suggest assessment strategies for the skills or content that are the focus of a particular lesson. PowerPoint provides animations, transitions, and graphics that are considered "cool tools" by students. Although these are helpful for motivating students to work on an assignment, they are often distracting. It is important for the teacher to direct learning by giving clear assessment criteria for work completed. Images must add to meaning, and text must be legible and of a suitable size. When students use the software for making presentations, animations and transitions should be used sparingly and only for a specific purpose.

Many of the projects include a checklist or rubric, and Excel files of these are included on the CD. Teachers can tailor these assessments to the needs of their class. Having a rubric specific to an assignment helps students understand what is required for successfully completing a task and gives them strategies for success. The rubric also helps educators identify and weight important aspects of the work.

There are many online resources to create rubrics. Rubistar (http://rubistar.4teachers. org) is an excellent resource, providing ready-made, modifiable rubrics on numerous topics. Teachers are encouraged to add further criteria to the assessments, based on their goals for a project. Nevertheless, I believe it is important not to try to perfect all possible criteria for evaluation for each assignment. It's better to be selective and direct younger students to focus their attention on one particular task. The teacher can customize the rubric, include the categories of his or her choice, and then change the point value and the definition of each category that is offered at each level. The rubric may then be saved or printed.

Higher Order Thinking Skills

This section lists the higher order thinking skills that students use while they learn content and do the assignments. Bloom's taxonomy ranks thinking skills from lowest to highest, as represented in Fig. 17.

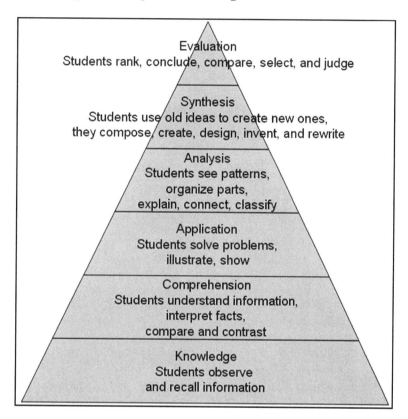

Figure 17. Bloom's taxonomy of higher order thinking skills

Computer Skills Practiced

This section lists the computer skills necessary to complete the assignment. Scaffolding helps students gradually develop their technology skills. Refer to the Scope and Sequence Chart of PowerPoint Skills at the end of the previous chapter for a list of these skills.

Subject Areas and Standards Addressed

This section lists the subject areas and standards that are addressed in each lesson. It also specifies the NETS for Students that are targeted in each lesson. The lessons in this book are particularly geared to help students gain the skills they need to meet these technology standards. Students develop skills and become proficient users of this productivity software. The skills they master easily transfer to other applications. They use PowerPoint to collaborate with others and to produce creative works. Students also use it to communicate ideas and information to a particular audience. In the course of the assignments, they develop their ability to use research tools and to complete tasks that involve problem solving and decision making.

Links to the U.S. education standards for technology and other subjects can be accessed at the Education World Web site at www.education-world.com/standards/national/.

Resources Needed

This section lists the materials that students will use to complete the lesson, including Web sites and books.

PowerPoint Activity

This section gives the teacher step-by-step instructions for how to complete the lesson. The detailed instructions are written for PowerPoint 2003; however all lessons can also be completed in PowerPoint 2007. PowerPoint 2007 has a significantly updated interface—toolbars have been replaced by the Ribbon—so please see appendix A for a list of most commonly used commands and where to access them.

Extensions and Modifications

This section details extension and modification ideas for the lesson. I hope teachers who use this book will be inspired to develop their own lessons based on the ideas presented.

As teachers use the lesson ideas in this book and then develop their own, they may choose to use the WKHPE table (Table 3) that I have adapted to plan and review student PowerPoint assignments.

Table 3. WKHPE table to help plan assignments

Decide what you want them to learn	Determine what students already know	Consider how they will find the information they need as they explore new ideas	Design the product(s) they will create to share what they have learned	Evaluate the learning and modify the assignment
Clarify Goals • Instructional/ curricular goals • Goals for fostering higher order thinking • Goals for developing research, writing, and technology skills	Plan a prompt to stimulate interest, formulate questions to elicit this information, think of ways to encourage brainstorming.	Decide how you can help make the information available and easily accessible to them.	Decide how to structure the product. Show them an example of the desired outcome. Demonstrate instructions. Present guidelines for evaluation, a rubric, or a checklist. Develop written instructions, or a template with formatting, questions, main ideas.	Examine whether you met your goals. Modify the assignment to better meet the goals and try it with a different group of students.

Lessons for Younger Students

Young students don't need to know how to use *all* the tools in PowerPoint. One assignment may require them to enter text in given text boxes and insert clip art, another to insert a photograph and write a sentence. Students develop these skills gradually. Kindergarteners and first graders use it on a limited basis. They may open and modify a template that structures the activity and guides learning, or they may open a blank presentation and use specific tools to complete an assignment. Teachers modify templates to suit instructional goals.

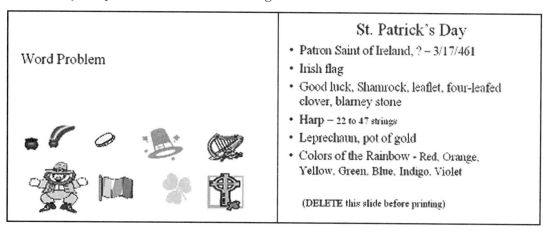

Figure 18. Students make up a word problem selecting from the clip art on the template to illustrate it. They use the vocabulary list on the last slide to help them.

At the start of the lesson, I model the computer skills, and then ask for volunteers to demonstrate the steps again to the class. Students help their neighbors if necessary. They are reminded to show or tell them, but not to do the job for them. Young students often need help opening and saving the appropriate file, but generally have no problem navigating from slide to slide. They also need adult assistance to make the right choice of printer and to print slides or handouts with a number of slides per page.

A disadvantage of using this program with early elementary students is that the drawing tools are not "kid friendly," and students experience some difficulty or frustration when they are required to select the tool each time, as the program does not remain in the drawing mode. If the primary purpose of the assignment is to draw, it is preferable to draw in a program such as Microsoft Paint, Kid Pix, or Scholastic Keys—a program that allows young students to use the MS Office applications with draw tools that are appropriately modified for them. Most assignments for younger students in this book do not involve drawing.

Young writers often communicate in non-verbal ways. PowerPoint provides visual methods of representing ideas and concepts, a bridge between the abstract and the concrete. This offers elementary school students the tools to communicate and think in new and meaningful ways. Students are engaged as they actively participate and create a PowerPoint product; they use higher order reasoning and become information producers. Their work on the computer is dynamic, allowing them to change and to improve on their ideas. Collaboration is facilitated, as the computer allows them to share information.

It is important to remember that students are not trying to perfect craftsmanship; rather they are using these tools for learning or communicating. Therefore, when they make a clay animation or a multimedia slide show, they accept that they must do the best that they can within a given time frame. For example, they learn quickly that it takes years of work and professional equipment to make a clay animation movie like one featuring the characters Wallace and Gromit, yet students do learn the basic technique and are excited by the creative challenge. Likewise, teachers who use the templates and lesson ideas in *PowerPoint Magic* also do not need to have a high level of expertise because their focus is on the educational purpose for using the tool.

Lessons At-a-Glance

Each lesson in this book is designed to address specific grade levels, subject areas, and higher order thinking skills, as illustrated in the following chart.

Lesson Title	Grade Level	Subject area					Higher Order Thinking Skills			
		ELA	M	SS	Sc	VA	Application	Analysis	Synthesis	Evaluation
Narrative Writing Lessons										
1. My First Stories	1–2	X						X	X	
2. Story Building	2–3	X						X	X	X
3. Halloween Stories	2	X							X	
4. Digital Storytelling	6–8	X						X	X	X
5. Visualize, Dramatize, and Retell a Story	5–6	X							X	X
Descriptive Writing Lessons										
6. What Do I See?	2	X			X		X	X		X
7. Guess Who I Am?	1–3	X					X		X	
8. Main Ideas and Details	5	X						X		X
Research Writing Lessons										
9. Celebrating Our Culture	3			X		X		X	X	
10. Penguins	3	X			X		X	X	X	X
11. The Year in Review	3, 6–8	X		X		X	X	X	X	X
12. Internet Research 101	7–8	X						X	X	X
Instruction Writing Lessons										
13. Shape Up!	1, 6	X	X				X	X	X	
14. A Day at the Gallery	5	X				X	X	X	X	
15. Presidents Day	1, 8	X		X				X	X	X
16. Clay Animation 101	4–8	X				X	X	X	X	
Persuasive Writing Lessons										
17. Buy Me!	3	X				X		X	X	X
18. Persuasive Paragraphs	5–8	X						X	X	X
Poetic Composition Lessons										
19. First Rhymes	1	X				X		X	X	
20. Mother's Day Poem	4–5	X						X	X	
21. Picturing Poetry	6–8	X						X	X	
Visualization and Graphic Representation Lessons										
22. Greater Than, Less Than, or Equal To?	1	X	X				X	X	X	X
23. Simple Machines	3	X			X			X	X	X

Narrative Writing Lessons
Digital Storytelling

Lesson 1 • My First Stories

Grades 1, 2

Lesson Description

Students create simple illustrated stories, incorporating words from a spelling list, by inserting text into a text box and using the Insert Clip Art button to insert pictures.

Students first read a story about animals with the teacher and identify the story elements: the title, who the story was about, what happened in the beginning, the most exciting part, and what happened in the end. They comment on the illustrations that help to convey meaning. Students then make up their own stories, using words from a spelling list, typing the text into a slide, and choosing pictures to illustrate it so that someone other than the student writer can read the story.

This assignment is completed in one lesson, and students do not need to fully develop their stories. Instead, they are being asked to practice and develop their writing skills on the computer. Students should be instructed to pay attention to conventions and try to begin each sentence with an uppercase letter and end each sentence with a period. Students highlight the spelling words in a different color and search the Clip Gallery for pictures. This search activity encourages students to pay careful attention to the correct spelling of words, as they can only locate the pictures if the words are spelled correctly. They may also browse the Clip Gallery and insert pictures in place of words they cannot yet spell. Students learn to use the right mouse button to help with spelling when they spell a word phonetically and it is consequently marked as misspelled (underlined on-screen with a wavy red line). Younger students often need adult help to select the correct spelling. When they have finished, students print their stories and read them to each other.

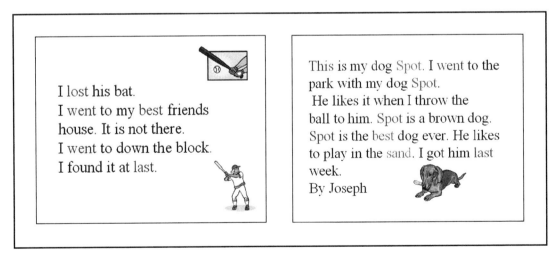

Figure 1.1 Spelling word stories written by students at the beginning of second grade.

Assessment

Students use the *Story with My Spelling Words* checklist to make sure they have completed all the elements required for the story. The checklist is provided on the CD as an Excel document that can be modified by the teacher.

Higher Order Thinking Skills	Computer Skills Practiced	Subject Areas and Standards Addressed
Analysis: Analyze the components of a story that is read to the class and discuss how it is organized. **Synthesis:** Create and share an original story that uses spelling words and pictures from either the Clip Gallery or photographs.	Insert text Insert clip art Change font color Right-click marked words for spelling suggestions	NETS•S: 1.a, b; 2.b; 4.b; 6.b English Language Arts: NL-ENG.K-12.4, .5

Resources Needed

List of spelling words provided by the teacher

Picture dictionary to help students spell search words for clip art

PowerPoint Activity

1. Students open a new blank presentation in PowerPoint and choose the Title Only slide layout (Fig. 1.2).

   - If the slide has the wrong layout, students can go to the Format menu and click on Slide Layout > Title Only to change it.

2. Students click on the text box to select it, then enter their text inside the box. Students may need instruction in how to use the Shift key to make an upper-case letter.

3. Students insert clip art into the slide. The clip art can then be resized or moved.

   - To insert clip art, students go to the Drawing toolbar and click on the Insert Clip Art button. They enter a descriptive word for the picture they are looking for in the search box and press Search. Students then select a picture from the search results and insert it into the slide, either by double-clicking it, or by single-clicking it and then pressing Insert.

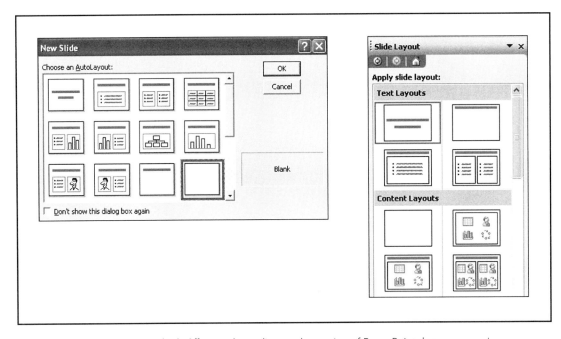

Figure 1.2 Layout options may look different, depending on the version of PowerPoint that you are using.

- To resize the picture proportionally, students click on a corner handlebar and, holding down the mouse button, drag it diagonally to the desired size. To move the picture within the slide, students click and hold down the mouse button in the center of the picture and drag it to the desired location.

4. Students highlight the spelling words and change them to a different color.

- To change the font color of a word, students first highlight the word, then go to the Formatting toolbar and click on the arrow next to the Font Color button and select the color of their choice.

5. Students look for misspelled words. If words are marked as misspelled (underlined with a red wavy line), students can get hints for correct spelling by right-clicking the underlined word. They then left-click on the correct option to replace the word.

6. Students print their story by going to the File menu and clicking on Print > Print What > Handouts > 2 slides per page > OK.

Extensions and Modifications

Chris Vogt, a first-grade teacher, had students take photographs and insert them as illustrations in an original story. The school purchased inexpensive digital cameras and students checked these out and took them home to take photographs. They were told to take five to ten photographs for a story that they would tell, on any topic of their choice. A short letter was sent home to parents, explaining that students should use the camera to take five photographs for a story that they would write up briefly at school. Some students who did not manage to save their pictures on the camera took their photographs at school. All students were allowed to supplement their photographs with clip art. As they inserted their pictures, students began writing their stories, one sentence per slide, in a new PowerPoint document. The teacher helped them insert the photographs. The stories were printed as 6-slides-per-page handouts; then students cut out the pages and stapled them together into small booklets.

To create the story pages:

1. Students open a new blank presentation in PowerPoint and choose the Title Only slide layout.

2. Students write the story title and their name on the first slide.

3. Students insert a new slide for each page of the book. They write one sentence per slide, then insert their photograph or clip art. Students will have to browse through the files on their computer to find the photographs they will use. They often need help locating the picture files the first time they do this. When they repeat the process, the program will automatically look in the same spot, whether it is on a CD or in a shared folder. Students can then move or resize the picture on the slide.

   - To insert a new slide, students go to the Insert menu and click on New Slide > Title Only.

4. Students print their story by going to the File menu and clicking on Print > Print What > Handouts > 6 slides per page > OK.

Lesson 2 • Story Building

Grades 2, 3

Lesson Description

Elementary students love to hear a good story. They also love to invent their own original stories. These students can be quite animated and have lots of imagination and ideas for single-event stories, yet as they begin to write more complex narratives, their stories often lack structure. The stories may include too many events and too little detail. As we know, writing a story is a complex task, and in this lesson students will consider, with guidance, how an author tells a good story and how it is structured.

Have students examine a story they have read and enjoyed. Help them identify and express the elements of a good story. Read excerpts from the book or from an online site (such as Amazon.com) that allows you to project the cover page, illustrations, and excerpts. One second-grade class suggested that the following elements make a good story: rhyming, humor, and interesting illustrations.

Identify the sequence of events and the elements of the story, using the *Story Building* template in Outline view to help students determine the setting; characters; problem; solution to the problem; and the ending. Students learn how the beginning of the story can entice the reader and lead them to read more.

Students then think up an original story and use colored crayons to make a picture that will tell the tale. They are strongly encouraged not to use television characters or stories, but to invent their own. Before they write, students get together with a partner and share the story orally. Next, they open the *Story Building* template in PowerPoint and write up and revise their first narrative. This template helps students structure their story and provides a space for them to work on each of the story elements. They could also use the *Three Tries* template, which provides the same structure as the *Story Building* template but asks students to describe three attempts to solve the problem instead of just one.

Using PowerPoint for this task allows students to compose in a nonlinear way, to jump back and forth, and to start with the part that interests them. They can add, delete, and rearrange ideas and sentences easier than if they were composing on paper. Easy access to pictures helps link verbal and visual images, stimulating creativity. The final draft of the story may or may not be written on the computer.

Assessment

Students use the *Original Story* checklist to help them focus on the structure of their story. The checklist is provided on the CD as an Excel document that can be modified by the teacher.

Higher Order Thinking Skills	Computer Skills Practiced	Subject Areas and Standards Addressed
Analysis: Analyze a familiar story, identify the parts. **Synthesis:** Predict the events in a story; invent an original story. **Evaluation:** Evaluate a story, select the parts that appeal to the reader.	Insert text in a text box, modify text Use the arrow key to move the insertion point Press the Insert key on the keyboard (with help from an adult) Highlight and delete text Insert clip art Print full-page slide, using Outline view page	NETS•S: 1.a, b; 2.b; 4.b; 6.b English Language Arts: NL-ENG.K-12.3, .5, .12

Resources Needed

Amazon.com Web site (www.amazon.com) for excerpts from stories, first pages, summaries, and sample illustrations

PowerPoint Activity

1. Depending on the type of story students will write, have them open the *Story Building* template (Fig. 2.1), or the *Three Tries* template (Fig. 2.2).

2. Students should replace the words already on the slides with their own words. To do this, they click on a slide to select it in the Outline pane, then click on the text box they want to change. The text box will have the handlebars showing if it is selected. Students click so that the cursor is showing, highlight the words they want to change, then enter the new words.

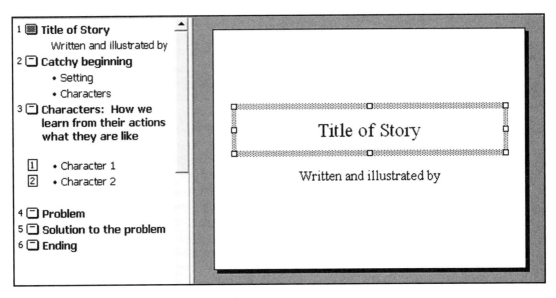

Figure 2.1 First page of the *Story Building* template.

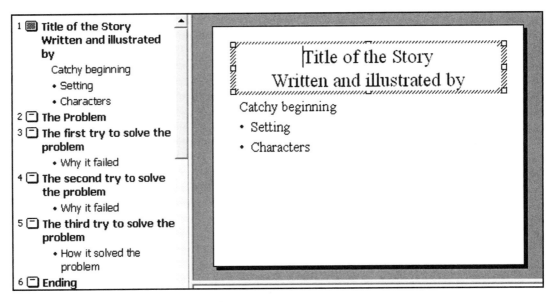

Figure 2.2 First page of the *Three Tries* template.

3. If the student wants to keep the existing words on the text box, they should make sure that nothing is highlighted. Instead, they put the cursor where they want the words to go, then enter the text. They can also use the arrow keys on the keyboard to move the cursor into position.

- If the computer is eating up the letters in front of the cursor when students enter new letters, they should press the Insert key on the keyboard. This acts like a toggle switch, and in one mode will *replace* the next letter with what it typed, and in the other mode will leave text ahead as is, *inserting* what is typed.

4. Students insert clip art into the slide. The clip art can then be resized or moved.

   - To insert clip art, students go to the Drawing toolbar and click on the Insert Clip Art button. They enter a descriptive word for the picture they are looking for in the search box and press Search. Students then select a picture from the search results and insert it into the slide, either by double-clicking it or by single-clicking it and then pressing Insert.

   - To resize the picture proportionally, students click on a corner handlebar and, holding down the mouse button, drag it diagonally to the desired size. To move the picture within the slide, students click and hold down the mouse button in the center of the picture and drag it to the desired location.

5. Students print their story outline by going to the File menu and clicking on Print > Print What > Handouts > 6 slides per page > OK. The outline will print on one page.

   See Figure 2.3 for an example of an original story written by a student using the *Three Tries* template.

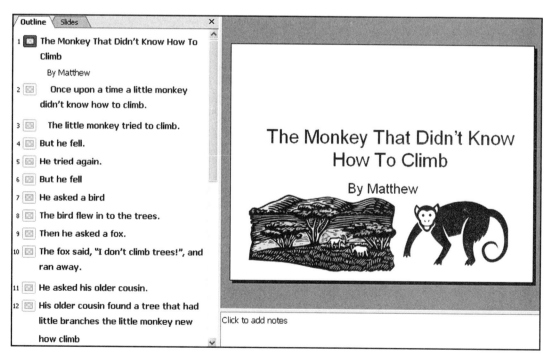

Figure 2.3 Story in development using the *Three Tries* template.

Extensions and Modifications

- Have students dress up as characters in the book and use a digital camera to take their photographs. Then have them write a story using the photographs and clip art.

- Students write a rebus story with pictures in place of some words. They may use pictures for words they don't know how to spell. They may write first and then select key words to replace with a picture every time that word occurs in the story.

- After sharing story ideas, the class selects the three stories they like best. Then they join with the authors to write the stories using words instead of pictures. Each student takes on a different role; they may each write a page, or some students may play the role of illustrator or editor.

Lesson 3 • Halloween Stories

Grade 2

Lesson Description

Students at our school dress up in costume on Halloween. This provides an opportunity to take photographs and encourage children to imagine stories about their characters.

The *Haunted Classroom* template sets the scene for the story—somebody has disappeared from the classroom and a costumed character has taken his or her place. Students are photographed in their costumes at their desks. The class discusses what they will each say about their character and brainstorms ideas for a good ending to the story.

Students modify the *Haunted Classroom* template to write a description of what their character looks like and does; insert their photograph; then write their own ending to the story. The template also provides a page for readers to write their comments.

The class selects the best of the writing to include in a final copy. This final copy may be stapled or bound together into a book that students can take turns taking home to share with their families. Family members provide feedback on the Comments by Readers for the Authors of this Book page at the back of the book.

A tiger is in the classroom today and Hugh has disappeared!

Figure 3.1 Students create a Halloween mystery story, combining their own pictures and text to create a collaborative class book.

Assessment

Students use the *Behind the Mask* checklist to check their own work. The checklist is provided on the CD as an Excel document that can be modified by the teacher.

Higher Order Thinking Skills	Computer Skills Practiced	Subject Areas and Standards Addressed
Synthesis: Collaborate to create a Halloween storybook; formulate clues for the reader to guess what photograph will be on the next page; invent a story and create an imaginative narrative; design photographs to convey meaning (in lesson extension).	Insert and delete text Insert clip art Insert, move, and resize a photograph Print full-page slides Format slide background (in lesson extension)	NETS•S: 1.a, b; 2.b; 4.b; 6.b English Language Arts: NL-ENG.K-12.4, .5, .12

Resources Needed

digital camera

PowerPoint Activity

1. Students open the *Haunted Classroom* template in PowerPoint.

2. They enter their name on Slide 1 then follow the prompts on the remaining slides to add and replace text. They click on the scroll bar to move to the next slide.

3. Students insert their photo in Slide 6. The photo can then be resized or moved.

   - To insert a photograph, students go to the Insert menu and click on Picture > From File. They must browse to find the picture where it is saved, possibly on a removable drive, a network, or in My Documents. They can either double-click the file or click on Insert to place the picture on the slide.

   - To resize the picture proportionally, students click on a corner handlebar and, holding down the mouse button, drag it diagonally to the desired size. To move the picture within the slide, they click and hold down the mouse button in the center of the picture and drag it to the desired location.

4. Students insert clip art into the slides. The clip art can then be resized or moved.

   • To insert clip art, students go to the Drawing toolbar and click on the Insert Clip Art button. They enter a descriptive word for the picture they are looking for in the search box and press Search. They then select a picture from the search results and insert it into the slide, either by double-clicking it, or by single-clicking it and then pressing Insert.

5. Students print their completed slide shows by going to the File menu and clicking on Print > OK.

Extensions and Modifications

Third or fourth graders, in preparation for Halloween, plan an original story with a group of two or three other students.

1. After sharing with the class what their costumes will be, students form groups to make a story. The group develops their story by discussing the story line and sketching six poses for photographs on a storyboard, which is printed from the *Blank Storyboard* template (Fig. 3.2). The template should be printed as Handouts (six slides per page). Instructions for students may be added in the header or footer.

2. Students make up a story with a beginning, middle, and end.

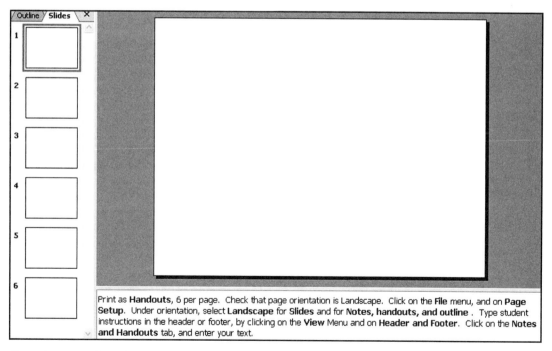

Figure 3.2 Screenshot of the *Blank Storyboard* template.

3. On the day that students are dressed up, they also bring along any props they will need for the photography sessions. They rehearse their poses, and groups take turns getting their pictures taken with a digital camera. It might be helpful to get parents to volunteer as photographers.

4. Students work as a group to publish their story. They insert their photographs into a PowerPoint slide show and briefly relate the story in a text box on each slide.

5. Groups share their slide shows with other groups in the class and then choose one story for which they will write only a beginning paragraph. A checklist for this part of the assignment would include items like:

   • We used our imagination to make the characters part of a plausible story. (Although the story is not real, it must be credible.)

   Extend this list to suit your students.

6. You may want to assign a writing project to enlist further student input on the introduction to the story. Have them describe the characters and setting. Remind them to have a catchy beginning, give a detailed description of the setting, and to describe the characters as they introduce them. The characters should be interesting and believable. Consider basing the assessment on the introduction writing project. Figure 3.3 shows slides from a story made by fourth-grade students.

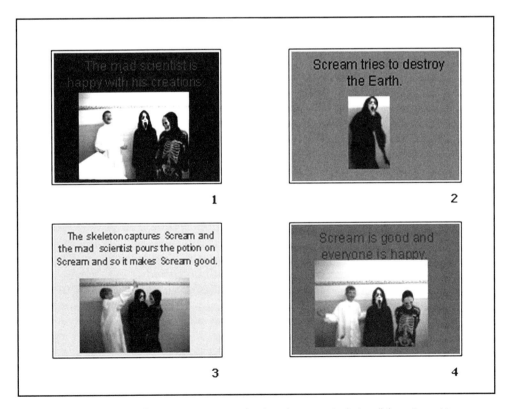

Figure 3.3 Students use Halloween costumes to develop characters in their collaborative writing.

Lesson 4 • Digital Storytelling

Grades 6–8

Lesson Description

Young students are typically imaginative, and they love to think up fantastical stories. In spite of their enthusiasm, their stories are often poorly organized, problems are not developed or resolved in a believable way, and characters are not fully developed. Writing and illustrating an original story is a complex task and students need structure to break down the steps for creating one. They also need guidance to improve the quality of their stories, helping them develop their characters and choose interesting problems with plausible solutions.

Initially, students should identify what they like about a story they have read. In a class discussion, students then analyze several models of a good children's story. In response to *Curious George*, students in my school identified the following story elements as appealing: title, likeable characters, interesting story, appealing pictures, and problems that they relate to. Students then skim through several sample picture books. They compare these books, identify the problems and how they are resolved, and then comment on how the story ends.

Students can use the *Story Concept Map* graphic organizer to analyze a story of their choice. Using this graphic organizer helps students identify a catchy beginning and how readers learn what the characters are like through actions, words, and thoughts. In this way, students can learn how character traits are *shown* in a story, rather than *told*.

Working with a partner, students use the same graphic organizer to start developing their own story. They can also use the *Character Development* graphic organizer to help develop their characters and the *Brainstorm Problems* graphic organizer to explore possible problems and choose the best.

Students plan their original story by writing up a storyboard in PowerPoint. They write the story outline in the Outline pane, entering each main idea on a new slide. In Slide Sorter view, they arrange, insert, and delete slides. They then begin writing, illustrating, and adding details in Slide view. The writing and illustrating processes happen simultaneously as students are inspired; the story changes as they draw and add pictures. Initially, students may choose to jot down key words or ideas and add details and write in paragraph format later, paying attention to writing and spelling conventions at that point. Students rewrite, revise, and even start over, improving quality and content as they go.

Students should create original illustrations for the story. They may use a combination of clip art, pictures they created themselves in a drawing program such as Kid Pix or Microsoft Paint, and elements they create with PowerPoint's drawing functions (AutoShapes, WordArt, etc.). These elements can be modified—rotated; grouped or ungrouped; layered; and the fill, font, line, and background colors can be changed using PowerPoint's drawing tools.

Some students spontaneously make drawings that radiate "Voice," which may be childlike, playful, and colorful. Even students who do not consider themselves talented artists can create fun pictures that convey meaning by copying clip art images, book illustrations, and cartoons. Using PowerPoint, students can also add labels and speech bubbles to help clarify their drawings and increase interest.

Student drawings improve when they give up trying to draw all the details and understand they can focus on key elements. Once students grasp this concept, they can, for example, focus on drawing only a lion's head instead of trying to draw a whole lion. Encourage students to give their drawings a personality by adding facial expressions and by paying attention to detail. See the *Illustration* checklist provided to see what elements you might use for assessment.

Each story is read and peer-reviewed using the *Peer Review* rubric, or teacher-reviewed using the *Teacher Evaluation* rubric. The evaluations are returned to the students, and students are allowed to edit their stories to improve them.

Finally, students share their books with a kindergarten audience.

In an extension activity, the young authors create a digital story and enhance it by inserting sound, animation, and interactivity into the PowerPoint slide show.

The following examples represent excerpts from storybooks written by sixth graders. "Conflict in the North Pole" is written in the style of the Berenstain Bears books: young characters argue; are urged to solve the problem by an adult (in this case a teacher); and then teacher and students work together to resolve the problem. Student authors chose original characters, setting, and problem. Students created original pictures using the drawing tools in PowerPoint. They grouped the separate pieces and resized the image to use in other slides.

Figure 4.1 Students drew original artwork to help tell the story of Billy the Penguin.

Others chose to write an original story, as shown in Figure 4.2. In that story, Dud the squirrel is in trouble for ignoring adult instructions and taking the golden nut from the bottom of the pile.

Figure 4.2 Students created and illustrated an original story.

One student, who was not often motivated to get his work done, wrote prolifically about Curious George going to the moon. He ended the PowerPoint slide show with a comment that succinctly describes the pattern in the *Curious George* series of books (Fig. 4.3).

Like all the other published Curious George books, it starts with curiousness, leads to mayhem, and ends just right. That may never change for Curious George, but its what he's always been doing, and what he will be doing for as long as he's a book.

Figure 4.3 One inspired young reader/author sums it all up.

Assessment

Each story is read and evaluated by every student in the class. Acting as evaluators, students use the *Peer Review* rubric to focus on the key elements of a good story; they look for evidence of these criteria in each picture book. When the evaluations have been filled out, they are returned to the student authors, who consider the feedback from peers. Student authors edit again to improve their stories.

The *Teacher Evaluation* rubric may also be used for this exercise. The rubric includes 15 criteria from which to calculate a grade. Excel will automatically calculate a percentage grade. This Excel document can be modified to add or delete criteria.

The rubrics are provided on the CD as Excel documents that can be modified by the teacher.

Higher Order Thinking Skills	Computer Skills Practiced	Subject Areas and Standards Addressed
Analysis: Analyze popular children's stories and identify the plot, characters, tone, and style of illustrations. **Synthesis:** Invent an original story designed for kindergartners. **Evaluation:** Students consider stories written by classmates, assess them on given criteria, and rank the stories.	Insert text, text boxes, WordArt Insert, move, resize, ungroup, delete parts, rotate, regroup, and duplicate clip art Use Draw tools or create an image in a drawing program and paste it into PowerPoint Print handouts two per page In the lesson extension: Insert music, voice recordings; animate graphics; and insert buttons with hyperlinks to additional slides	NETS•S: 1.a, b; 2.b; 4.b; 6.b English Language Arts: NL-ENG.K-12.4, .5, .12

Resources Needed

Drawing software such as Kid Pix, Microsoft Paint, Scholastic Keys, or Appleworks Paint

PowerPoint Activity

1. Students open a new blank presentation in PowerPoint. They choose an Auto Layout with Title Only to place a text box on each slide.

2. Students write an outline for the story, working in the Outline pane. To change the order of slides, they switch to Slide Sorter view and drag slides to move them into order.

3. Students go to Slide view to add details in the text box for each page of the book.

4. Students can edit text within the text box by dragging and dropping words or sentences. They should format the font, color, and size to reflect the meaning of words. They should also look for any words that are marked as misspelled and right-click them to choose the correct spelling option.

5. Students insert their illustrations (WordArt, clip art, and drawings). Students can then use PowerPoint's drawing tools to manipulate the graphics in many different ways to create the effects that they want.

   - To modify clip art, students click on the artwork to select it, then go to the Drawing toolbar and click on Draw > Ungroup. If they get a message asking to convert the object to a Microsoft Office Drawing Object, they should click OK. Students can then select any part of the artwork and change it—resize, fill with a color, or delete it.

   - To regroup parts of clip art, students drag the mouse over the pieces so that they are selected and their handlebars are showing, then go to the Drawing toolbar and click on Draw > Regroup.

   - To change the fill color of any element, students click on a graphic to select it, go to the Drawing toolbar then click on the arrow next to the Fill Color button and select a different color. To change a line color, they go to the Drawing toolbar then click on the arrow next to the Line Color button and select a different color.

   - To add AutoShapes and Lines, students select a tool by dragging the tool with the mouse onto the slide.

   - To rotate a drawing or clip art, students click on the artwork to select it, making sure the handlebars are showing, then click on the Free Rotate button. The artwork can then be rotated using the handlebars.

   - To layer graphics and text, students click on an object to select it, go to the Drawing toolbar, click on Draw, then select Bring to Front, Send to Back, Bring Forward or Send Backward.

   - To duplicate a picture, students click on the picture to select it, then hold down the CTRL button on the keyboard and press the "D" key once.

- To insert a speech bubble, students go to the Drawing toolbar and click on Autoshapes > Callouts. They click on the style of Callout they want, then click on the slide to place the bubble. The speech bubble can be resized and moved like other graphics. To change the fill color, students right-click the bubble to open the Format AutoShape dialog box, then select the color of their choice. To finish, they click inside the callout to enter text.

- To format a background for a slide, students right-click the slide and then left-click on Slide Background. Students then pull down on the arrow to select a color, or click on More Colors or Fill Effects for more options (Fig. 4.4). They then click Apply to apply this color to the current slide only, and Apply to All to apply the background to all slides in the slide show.

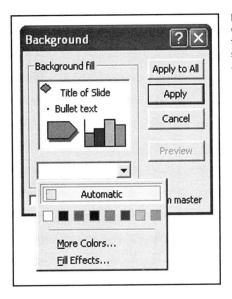

Figure 4.4 This dialog box opens when you right-click a slide to format the background, and students can select a color and a fill effect.

Extensions and Modifications

Students add sound and animation to create an audio book. Music can help set the tone of the story, or the story may be read aloud and recorded by the author.

Voice recording

To record voice, a microphone must be hooked up to the computer, or there must be an internal microphone to record sound.

1. Students go to the Start menu and click on All Programs > Accessories > Entertainment > Sound Recorder.

2. They click on the red button to record.

3. Students play the sound back and adjust the audio.

4. When they are happy with their recording, they save it by going to the File menu and clicking on Save. The audio will save as a .WAV document.

Inserting sound into the slide show

1. Students insert the sound by going to the Insert menu and clicking on Movies and Sound > From File. They then browse to locate the sound file and then click on Insert. They can also select From Gallery for prerecorded sounds and music, or visit Clips Online to get access to a large library of sound files on the Microsoft Web site.

2. Students determine if they want the sound to play on a mouse click, or on a "mouse over." To set up this action, they right-click the sound icon on the slide, then click on Action Settings in the dialog box. They can then choose the Mouse Click tab or the Mouse Over tab, and then check Object Action.

Adding animation to a slide show

Students add animation in Slide view, but to view animation they must be in Slide Show view.

1. Students click on the object they want to animate. They go to the Slide Show menu and click on Custom Animation. In the Custom Animation dialog box that pops up (Fig. 4.5), students click on the Effects tab then make their selection. They can then click on the Preview button to preview the effect.

2. After they have animated one or more objects, students click on the Order and Timing tab of the Custom Animation box to set an order for animations and sounds. Here, they can click on an animation event to select it, and under Start Animation they select whether to start the animation automatically by checking Automatically; then select a time lapse, or they can choose On Mouse Click.

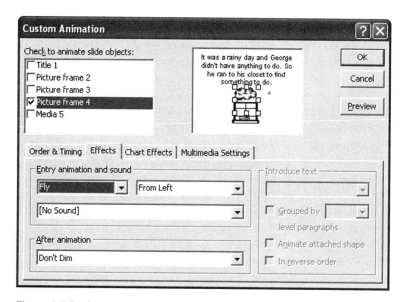

Figure 4.5 Students inserted animated clip art, which showed it raining. They grouped the raining cloud with their own original drawing of George peeking out the window.

Making a story interactive with hyperlinks

Students can make their story interactive by inserting action buttons with hyperlinks to other slides. Students can write a few possible endings to their story, and use the action buttons to hyperlink to these alternate endings. They can place action buttons over key words or graphics that lead the reader to more detailed information. There is also an action button that will take the reader back to the previously viewed slide.

- To add an action button to a slide, students right-click an object, clip art, or drawing. In the dialog box that appears, they click on Action Settings, then either on the Mouse Click or Mouse Over tab. They then click on Hyperlink, then Slide. At this point, all the slides will show up, and they select the one that they want to correlate with this link, and click OK (Fig. 4.6). A preview of the slide they select will show up in the window.

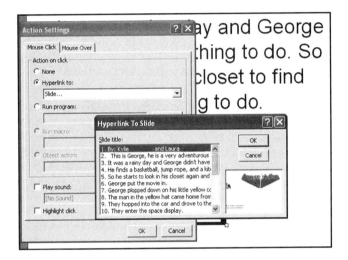

Figure 4.6 To get this screen, right-click a picture, click on Action Settings, check Hyperlink to and click on Slide.

- To add a Back button to a slide, students go to the Standard toolbar and click on Slide Show, then Action Button. They select the button style of their choice, and drag the mouse on the slide to draw the button. The Action Settings dialog box automatically pops up and they choose to Hyperlink to Last Slide Viewed. This action takes the reader back to the place they were in the story before they clicked on the hyperlinked button. Or, if the slide is the end of the story, the link could lead the reader to a "The End" slide—first make this slide, then choose to Hyperlink the button to it.

- To place an invisible button over the whole page, students go to the Standard toolbar, click on Slide Show, then Action Buttons. They select the Custom action button and use their mouse to draw a rectangle over the slide (Fig. 4.7).

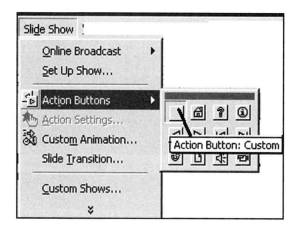

Figure 4.7 Students select a Custom Action Button and draw this over the selected area on the slide where they want the button to appear.

A green button will appear on top of the slide. Students double-click the button and the Format Autoshape box will open. Under Fill Color, they select No Fill; under Line Color, they select No Line. The button will be invisible. Students can try it out by viewing the slide show in Slide view.

Lesson 5 • Visualize, Dramatize, and Retell a Story

Grades 5, 6

Lesson Description

Student readers share pictures they have in their heads when reading a particular story. In this lesson, they dramatize an incident from a story using real photographs and their imagination to modify reality as they change scale and create backdrops.

Students are instructed to stick to the ideas and content of the story. As actors in the scene, students dress in costume and take photographs of one another in front of a plain, monotone backdrop, wall, or curtain. Then students "enhance" the photographs on the computer. Working in a paint program, they select only the outline of themselves and delete the background in the photograph. Next, in PowerPoint, they combine their photographs with clip art and other graphics to add props and a backdrop, and to change the scenery. They can resize, enlarge, minimize, duplicate, and animate images.

The object of this assignment is not to perfect the skills for producing professional artwork, but to explore the exciting possibilities of using graphics to communicate creative ideas.

In this example, students chose to focus on a chapter of *The Phantom Tollbooth*. Inspired by the Lethargians in the book, students inserted speech bubbles and WordArt into their pictures, and then resized images to "shrink" people to smaller than hand-size (Fig. 5.1).

Figure 5.1 Students can shrink themselves and create pictures that modify reality by resizing actual photographs.

But the possibilities for this lesson don't end with manipulating images. Students can also include a quote from the story or chapter that they have selected to clearly show the author's intention. Students then finish off this project by making a slide that explains the lesson learned from their story or a story chapter (Fig 5.2).

From this section of <u>The Phantom Tollbooth</u> we learned that jumping to conclusions wastes a lot of time and that the way to avoid it is to have knowledge.

Figure 5.2 Students explain what they learned from reading their story.

Assessment

Students use the *Retell a Story* checklist to check their own work. The checklist is provided on the CD as an Excel document that can be modified by the teacher.

Higher Order Thinking Skills	Computer Skills Practiced	Subject Areas and Standards Addressed
Analysis: Read text and explain with photographs and pictures; analyze text and infer the author's intention. **Synthesis:** Create a dramatization of the text.	Take digital photographs, open and crop them in a paint program Insert clip art and photographs from a file Layer or order graphics Insert speech bubbles	NETS•S: 1.a, b; 2.a, b, d; 4.b; 6.b English Language Arts: NL-ENG.K-12.2, .3, .4

PowerPoint Activity

1. Students open a new blank presentation in PowerPoint and choose the Title Only slide layout.

2. On the first slide, students create a title slide with the book title, author, page numbers of the extract, and names of the group members.

3. Students insert a new slide, choosing a Text Box format. Students select an important quote from the book and insert it into this new slide. They should be instructed to enter the quote in quotation marks.

4. Students insert a new slide for each of the photographs. They first make a backdrop for the characters using clip art, or students may prefer to create an original picture in Paint, AppleWorks, or Kid Pix and paste it onto the slide. Students can then layer the elements and insert speech bubbles.

   - To selectively crop parts of the photos, students can use the Microsoft Paint program. They go to the Start menu and click on Accessories > Paint. In Paint, they go to the File menu and click on Open to open the photograph. Students should click on the Free-Form Select button on the Toolbox, then hold down the mouse button and drag over the outline of what they want to select. They can go to the View menu and select Zoom > Large Size to enlarge the picture and make it easier to select details. To return to regular size, they select Zoom > Normal Size. From Paint, they can copy their selection and paste it onto a slide in PowerPoint.

   - To layer one picture on top of the other, students click on the picture so that it is selected, then go to the Drawing toolbar and click on Order, then Bring to Front.

   - To insert a speech bubble, students go to the Drawing toolbar and click on Autoshapes, then Callouts. They click on their selection and drag the mouse onto the slide to make the speech bubble. They click inside the bubble to insert text.

Extensions and Modifications

Students complete the same PowerPoint activity using a chapter or incident from a fantasy novel of their choice. They visualize the scenes, analyze and clarify the meaning and author's intention, select an important quote and create the slide show.

Descriptive Writing Lessons
Explain and Clarify

Lesson 6 • What Do I See?

Grade 2

Lesson Description

Students use digital photographs to document their learning, and these visual cues stimulate writing as they present their findings. Elementary students experience tremendous excitement the first time they use the digital camera, and this motivates them to share what they see and then write as they reflect on their observations. This lesson asks students to reflect on a science experiment with fruits and seeds. The extensions provide more ideas for students using digital cameras to record their observations: they taste apples on Johnny Appleseed day; identify, photograph, and describe colors; and record observations from a field trip.

Students take photographs as they cut up pieces of fruit, then remove, count, and examine the seeds. The *Fruit and Seeds* template sets up a slide show for students to insert photographs they have taken of their investigation of seeds and fruits. Students label the photographs and include their observations on each slide. They can find additional information, such as where the fruits are grown, from an online encyclopedia such as the World Book Encyclopedia Online (www.worldbookonline. com). Alternately, the teacher can print the slide show, and students take home the printouts and write a sentence next to each slide to document their findings about the fruit.

Students use the *Fruit and Seeds* template's graphic organizer, in the form of a comparison table, to compare and classify the fruits. This slide may be printed for students to write on as they make their observations. The template also provides a slide to write a short paragraph to summarize discoveries and draw conclusions.

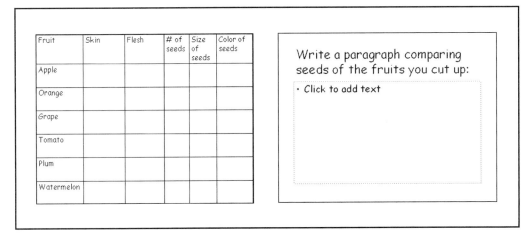

Figure 6.1 Students use a table in PowerPoint to organize and compare information from their classroom observations. They then write a paragraph to summarize their findings. If using a hard copy to complete the exercise is more suitable, the "Click to add text" portion of the slide can be deleted before printing.

Assessment

Students complete the *Fruit and Seeds* checklist to help guide them in this activity. The checklist is provided on the CD as an Excel document that can be modified by the teacher.

Higher Order Thinking Skills	Computer Skills Practiced	Subject Areas and Standards Addressed
Analysis: Explain classroom activities by referring to photographs. **Application:** Relate what is observed to prior knowledge, or to information in books, or to online sources. **Evaluation:** Students evaluate photographs that have been taken, and select to insert in their slide show; students compare their findings about the different fruits; students support their findings with online and print references.	Insert text Insert a photograph from file Browse photographs to select an appropriate one Move from cell to cell in a table Print handouts two per page, six per page, or three per page with lines	NETS•S: 2.b; 3.d; 5.b English Language Arts: NL-ENG.K-12.8, .12 Science: NS.K-4.3 LIFE SCIENCE

Resources Needed

Fruit

Digital camera

Online encyclopedia; World Book online encyclopedia (www.worldbookonline.com) is recommended

PowerPoint Activity

1. Students open the *Fruit and Seeds* template.

2. Students add their name to the first slide.

3. On the following slides, students insert their photographs of the fruit. The pictures can then be resized.

    *   To insert a photograph, students go to the Insert menu and click on Picture > From File to place a photograph on the slide. They can resize the picture by clicking on it to highlight it, clicking on a corner handlebar, and dragging from corner to corner.

4. Students add text to each slide to record their observations.

5. Students enter information about each fruit in the comparison table, and then write a short summary paragraph on the last slide.

6. Students print their slide show by going to the File menu and clicking on Print > Print What > Handouts > 2 slides per page > OK.

Extensions and Modifications

*   **Apple-tasting on Johnny Appleseed Day.** Students taste apples, then discuss, compare, and rank them. The *Apples* template provides students with a handout that they use to record their findings as they taste the types of apples and rank their favorites. The teacher may use the photographs of apples already in the template, or take photographs of the apples students will taste that day, and insert them in their place, deleting unneccessary slides. The slide show can be printed three per page so that students can make notes about each apple as they taste it. Students keep a written record on the lines next to the pictures where they label each type of apple. The final slide, which is the table for naming the apples, describing what they taste like, and ranking them (Fig. 6.2) may be printed out as a full page slide for students to write on. The table is completed with comparisons of the taste of the apples, and students rank the fruit from most to least favorite. Class discussion about what each one tastes like gives students the vocabulary to describe the taste. The ranking outcomes for favorite apple can be tallied, and students can chart the class findings using Excel.

Name of apple	What it tastes like	My ranking
Gala	Very sweet	1
Red delicious	Dry, but sweet	6
Yellow delicious	Plain, not much flavor	5
Macintosh	Sour!	3
Jonathan	Sour but good	4
Granny Smith	Tart and crisp	2

Apples

By Tommy

I am wearing a Johnny Appleseed hat.

The apple tastes good.

Figure 6.2 Students create an apple-tasting score card, and they can make a booklet that includes a photograph of them tasting the apples.

- Print a worksheet with slides showing photographs taken by students, and have them write a sentence about each picture and name a color shown in it. Print three per page with lines next to the pictures, so that students can write sentences on those lines for homework. Students can use Enchanted Learning's I Love Colors Web page (www.enchantedlearning.com/colors/) to identify colors and learn their correct spelling. There is a subscription cost for this Web site.

- Take a digital camera on a field trip and have students describe the place they visited and the people they met. Use photographs inserted into PowerPoint slides to help them reflect on what they did. Class brainstorming will help students develop vocabulary and clarify their ideas for this writing assignment.

Lesson 7 • Guess Who I Am?

Grades 1, 3

Lesson Description

Students introduce themselves to their peers at the beginning of the school year. They use pictures and words to describe themselves, responding to the prompts on the *Guess Who I Am* template. Students share information about their families, their best friends, their favorite color, book, toy, and food; they talk about their hero or what they want to be when they grow up. Finished projects are displayed, and students read about each other and then try to guess who the mystery person is before looking at the photograph or name on the last page of the booklet.

The *Guess Who I Am* template allows students to express themselves using pictures. They do not write original sentences but complete and modify sentences or phrases that are written for them. This gives them a restricted period of time to communicate about themselves. It helps students who are not prolific writers. They get some experience writing but are not overwhelmed by the task, and they are extremely proud of the professional-looking booklets that they print out.

Students who are beginning writers click on the appropriate slide and personalize the sentence as they complete it. They then find and insert meaningful clip art to illustrate their sentence.

Older students make their own slide show. They should be instructed to pay careful attention to style as well as content. These students may choose to create pictures in a drawing program such as Kid Pix, then copy the pictures and paste them into the PowerPoint slide show. They use the outline provided by a prompt on each slide to write sentences or a paragraph. They paste the pages of the booklet together in staggered fashion so that the topics show at the bottom of each page. The last page of the booklet includes a photograph of the author, allowing the reader to guess who the person is.

Figure 7.1 Younger students modify the template and illustrate their mini-autobiographies with clip art in PowerPoint, while upper-level elementary students create a new slide show in PowerPoint and use Kid Pix to create illustrations.

Assessment

Students complete the *Grade 1 Guess Who I Am* or *Grade 3 Guess Who I Am* check-list, as appropriate, to help guide them in this activity. The checklists are provided on the CD as Excel documents that can be modified by the teacher.

Higher Order Thinking Skills	Computer Skills Practiced	Subject Areas and Standards Addressed
Application: Students apply their knowledge about themselves to communicate with friends. **Synthesis:** Students design the pages of an original book about themselves.	Insert text Insert, move, and resize clip art Copy a picture from a graphic program like Kid Pix or AppleWorks and paste it onto a slide Print handouts two per page (with help from an adult)	NETS•S: 1.b, 2.b; 6.b English Language Arts: NL-ENG.K-12.5

Resources Needed

Drawing software such as Kid Pix, Microsoft Paint, Scholastic Keys or Appleworks Paint

PowerPoint Activity

1. Students open the *Guess Who I Am* template in PowerPoint.

2. Students click on Slide 1 on the Outline pane, then add pictures to the slide. The pictures can be resized and moved.

    *   To insert clip art, students go to the Drawing toolbar and click on the Insert Clip Art button. They enter a descriptive word for the picture they are looking for in the search box and press Search. Students then select a picture from the search results and insert it into the slide, either by double-clicking it, or by single-clicking it, then pressing Insert.

    *   To resize the picture proportionally, students click on a corner handlebar and, holding down the mouse button, drag it diagonally to the desired size. To move the picture within the slide, students click and hold down the mouse button in the center of the picture and drag it to the desired location.

Figure 7.2 Students use the prompt on each slide of the template to write a full sentence.

3. Students click on Slide 2 on the Outline pane. They click the slide to add text and insert pictures. They continue doing this with the rest of the slides (Fig. 7.2).

4. Students delete one slide they do not want to include in their booklet.

    •   To delete a slide, students click on that slide in the Outline pane, then press the Delete key on the keyboard.

5. Students insert their name and photograph into the last slide. The picture can be moved by dragging it.

    •   To insert the photograph, students go to the Insert menu and click on Picture > From File. They must then browse to find the photograph. They click the file they want, then click the Insert button.

6. Students save the slide show.

7. Students print their slide show by going to the File menu and clicking on Print > Print What > Handouts > 2 slides per page > OK.

8. Students cut out the pages and staple them together to make a booklet.

Extensions and Modifications

- Students who cannot find appropriate clip art, or students who are unable or unwilling to draw on the computer and paste from a drawing program into PowerPoint, can print the slides and draw with markers or crayons on the hard copy.

- Have students dress up as what they want to be when they grow up, such as a doctor, a teacher, a veterinarian, and so forth. Teachers then have students pose as if they are doing the job and take their photograph. Insert this on a slide entitled, "When I grow up I want to be a ..."

Figure 7.3 Student demonstrates how she will look as a teacher in the future.

If students include their photograph on the slide of their future career, have them enter only their name on the last slide, without a photograph. They should resize their name to make it very large and centered on the slide.

Students may be expected to write a paragraph with details about some of their ideas about the future. For example:

"When I grow up, I want to be a singer. The reason I chose this career is because I love to sing. I could sing all day. Singing is my passion. Whenever I am feeling sad, I go to my room and sing. Sometimes I make up songs too. This is what I want to be when I grow up."

Lesson 8 • Main Ideas and Details

Grade 5

Lesson Description

Students interview each other to get to know each other better. They make up questions to ask each other about likes and dislikes and what makes them unique or special. They ask their interviewees to give examples, or explain with a personal story, about their lives. The interviewers jot down details and phrases to include in the description as they talk and listen. They also take a picture of the interviewee in a typical pose, to add visual interest to their verbal description.

In preparation, the class brainstorms vocabulary that could be used to describe a person. Students then write a portrait describing their friend, focusing on the person's unique personality, hobbies, and talents. The *Describe a Person* template provides prompts for students to write their sentences and paragraphs. It gives them an outline to help them structure the paragraph. They begin with the main ideas in the Outline pane and then add details on each slide.

After completing the writing, students can either print the slide show as a booklet, placing a photograph of the person they describe on the last page, or they can send the outline to Microsoft Word. In Word, each slide forms a new paragraph, and the slide heading is centered. Students delete unnecessary text, revise to improve their writing using the spelling and grammar checker and the thesaurus, and then put the text into paragraph format.

> I'm unlike any other when it comes to my personality. Something that makes me an individual is I'm slow but neat. I may be shy, but I get mostly As on my report card. I don't like to say it, but I get annoyed easily especially when my sister bugs me.
>
> My personality

Figure 8.1 Sample slide completed by a student who describes the personality of a friend.

The last slide in the *Describe a Person* template provides guidelines for making a flipbook where the pages are layered with only the heading at the bottom of the page showing. This makes a pleasing display that entices the reader to lift the pages and read the details. Students begin by stapling or pasting slide seven on the line above number 7 on the printed copy of the slide shown in Figure 8.2.

1
2
3
4
5
6
7

Figure 8.2 Students cut out the slides for the booklet and paste them on the lines to make a flipbook. The pages will be staggered, showing the topic for each page at the bottom.

Students continue in that fashion, stapling slide 6 so that it lines up with the line above the number 6, until the pages are lined up one over the other, with page one on the top and the title of each page showing at the bottom of the page above it. The guidelines page may be stapled to a piece of construction paper to make a border around all the pages.

Assessment

The *Descriptive Paragraphs* rubric may be used for assessment purposes. In this rubric the weighting of the meaning, relevance, and logical order of ideas is different. The rubric is provided on the CD as an Excel document that can be modified by the teacher.

Higher Order Thinking Skills	Computer Skills Practiced	Subject Areas and Standards Addressed
Analysis: Students analyze their own unique qualities; analyze and classify their ideas, organizing them into a hierarchical structure of main ideas and details. **Evaluation:** Students compare themselves to other people and identify how they are different and unique.	Enter text and run the spelling checker Insert a photograph from file Send the words in a slide show outline to a Microsoft Word document In the extension lesson, students print the slide show in Notes view In the extension lesson, students insert animations, transitions, backgrounds, WordArt	NETS•S: 1.a, b; 2.b; 3.a, b, c; 4.c; 6.b English Language Arts: NL-ENG.K-12.4, .5, .12

Resources Needed

Digital camera

PowerPoint Activity

1. Students open the *Describe a Person* template in PowerPoint.

2. Students enter text on the first slide to make a title for their writing.

3. Students double-click on the text "Introduction here" to highlight these words so they will delete when they type, and write an introductory sentence.

4. Students decorate this slide with a border.

    • To add a border, students go to the Drawing toolbar and click on the Insert Clip Art button. They enter "borders" in the search box and press Search. Students then select a border from the search results and insert it into the slide, either by double-clicking it or by single-clicking it, then pressing Insert. Studenst can also insert pictures or shapes to make their own border.

5. Students modify the headings and add details about the person they are describing in the text boxes on the next six slides.

6. Students insert a photograph on the "Guess who I am…" slide. The photo can then be resized or moved.

- To insert a photograph, they go to the Insert menu and click on Picture > From File. They must browse to find the picture where it is saved, possibly on a removable drive, a network, or in My Documents. They can either double-click the file or click on Insert to place the picture on the slide.

- To resize the picture proportionally, students click on a corner handlebar and, holding down the mouse button, drag it diagonally to the desired size. To move the picture within the slide, students click and hold down the mouse button in the center of the picture and drag it to the desired location.

7. Students save and print their work. Students print their booklet by going to the File menu and clicking on Print > Print What > Handouts > 2 slides per page > OK.

8. To send the slide show to a Microsoft Word document, students go to the File menu and click on Send To > Microsoft Word. They then select Outline only to export text only, and click on OK. A Microsoft Word document, like the one shown in Figure 8.3, will open and text from titles and text boxes will be on the slides.

9. Students delete headings and change the writing to paragraph format. To do this, they highlight and delete words they do not want in the paragraph, such as the headings. They click the mouse to show the cursor next to the text they need to move up, and then press the backspace key.

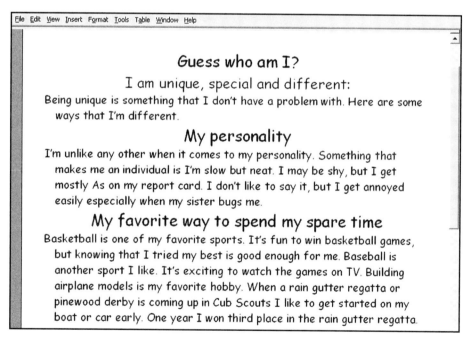

Figure 8.3 This is the Microsoft Word document that was created by writing on individual slides in a PowerPoint presentation first, after it was sent to Word in Outline format. The title of each slide is in a larger font, and each new slide is placed in a new paragraph.

Extensions and Modifications

- Students modify the *Main Idea and Details* template for other writing assignments. The ideas and details can be exported to Microsoft Word and printed in paragraph format. The *Main Ideas and Details* template helps students organize their ideas in hierarchical fashion, as they begin by noting the main ideas in outline format, then add details about that idea on individual slides (Fig. 8.4). This could be used as is, or modified to include other specific main ideas for writing on any topic across the curriculum.

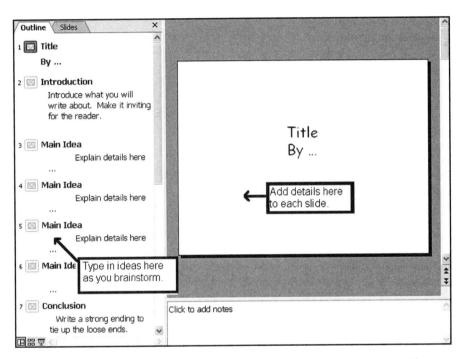

Figure 8.4 The *Main Idea and Details* template helps students structure their writing. They click on the Outline tab where they brainstorm main ideas, then add details to each slide.

- **Oral Presentation.** Students who write about themselves can make a slide show for presentation to an audience. Rather than utilizing their written paragraphs, they will communicate the main ideas of the slides they used to draft their paragraphs. They use words, pictures, photographs, speech bubbles, WordArt, colored backgrounds, and custom animation to enhance their spoken message. Details are written as Speaker Notes in the Notes pane, and the presenter uses these notes when he or she presents the slides. Speaker Notes may be written in outline format, using numbers or bullets to organize information and bold, italics, and underline to draw attention to important information. The slide show is printed in Notes view for use by the speaker.

  To print Notes Pages, students go to the File menu and click on Print > Print What > Notes Pages > OK.

- **Wanted Poster.** Students use the digital camera to take full-face and profile photographs, like mug shots for a "Wanted" poster. This is a fun activity that allows students to introduce themselves at the beginning of the school year. They describe their strengths and weaknesses, physical characteristics, likes, dislikes, and pastimes.

  The *Wanted Poster* template helps student structure their writing for the poster, and it encourages them to include a variety of factors in the description.

  To begin the PowerPoint presentation, students open the *Wanted Poster* template, then go to the Insert menu, click on Picture, then From File, and then click Browse to find the photographs they want to insert. When the picture is selected and the handlebars are showing, they drag the handlebars from corner to corner to shrink the photograph. They may also use the cropping tool on the Picture toolbar to crop the photograph. Headings may be formatted in bold. Students type in their descriptions, using complete sentences.

WANTED

Aliases: Becca, Becky
Description: She is 10 years old, has blond hair and blue eyes. She is 4' 8" tall.
Occupation: volleyball player, basketball player, gymnast, decorator, and student.
She has recently been seen in California, Wisconsin, Florida, Minnesota, Illinois, and Dominican Republic.
Interests: Her favorite thing to do is to hang out with friends. She likes to read and to go to movies
Dislikes: This girl does not like school that much.
Rewards of knowing her: If you know her you will have lots of fun. She is very talkative and fun to be around.
Caution: She talks too much, and she can sometimes be annoying. She is cranky when tired, and has a messy room

Figure 8.5 Sample Wanted Poster made by a student.

- **Certificates and awards.** Students can also make certificates or awards documents. A Best Person award gives an opportunity to express gratitude. An example of this kind of award is a Best Mom or Best Dad award. Students can also use these certificates to affirm their own worth, making one for themselves. Students decorate the page with a border, add clip art, use adjectives to describe the person, and write approximately five reasons why the person deserves the award.

Research Writing Lessons
Investigate and Explore

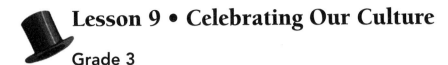

Lesson 9 • Celebrating Our Culture

Grade 3

Lesson Description

Third-grade students develop pride in their own cultural heritage and learn to understand and respect the cultural diversity of our society as they compare celebrations in different communities. Students share information about their own heritage and special celebrations they have in their families. They describe how they honor their ancestors and their family history with their classmates.

The teacher opens the *Cultural Celebrations* template and projects it on a large screen for students to brainstorm ideas and share what they know about the holidays. Web resources can be accessed to supplement what students already know. As students make suggestions, the information is added to the template. The template includes St. Patrick's Day, Cinco de Mayo, and Kwanzaa. Different celebrations can be inserted, depending on the students' suggestions.

Cinco de Mayo

- Celebrate our heritage
- Date:
- Clothes, Food, Decorations
- Parades/Special celebrations

Figure 9.1 Sample *Cultural Heritage* template

The class selects three celebrations to compare. Information shared by students may be printed as handouts for the class to use when they make their selections. The teacher reviews the activity on the large screen, and explains what goes in each circle and how they intersect. Students use the *Celebration Comparison* template to compare the holidays. This graphic organizer helps them organize and compare ideas. Students enter information about the three holidays in the intersecting sections (Fig. 9.2). They format font and color and add clip art to enhance their written communication. This template can be modified to include different holidays.

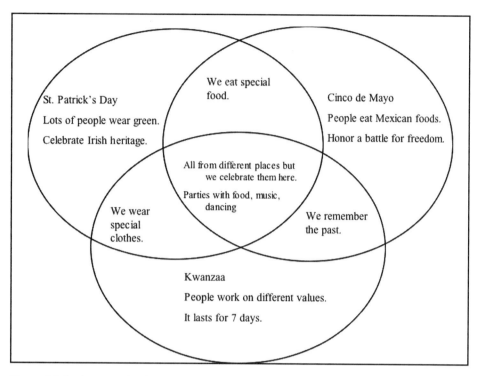

Figure 9.2 Student sample of a Venn diagram comparing cultural celebrations.

Students who have slow keyboarding skills may be allowed to print a copy with a picture and holiday heading in each circle, and then write their information with a pencil on the hard copy.

Assessment

Students complete the *Celebrating Our Heritage* checklist to help guide them in this activity. The checklist is provided on the CD as an Excel document that can be modified by the teacher.

Higher Order Thinking Skills	Computer Skills Practiced	Subject Areas and Standards Addressed
Comprehension: Select and interpret facts found in an encyclopedia for the purpose of learning about cultural celebrations. **Analysis:** Analyze and compare the way holidays are celebrated; organize ideas on a Venn diagram. **Synthesis:** Combine and integrate knowledge about a variety of cultural holidays.	Undo the previous step on computer Insert text box Change font color Insert and resize clip art Print full-page slide Enter query in search text box online	NETS•S: 1.a, b; 2.b; 3.b, c Social Studies: NSS-USH. K-4.1 Visual Arts: NA-VA.9-12.3

Resources Needed

Online encyclopedia; World Book online encyclopedia (www.worldbookonline.com) is recommended

PowerPoint Activity

1. Students open the *Celebration Comparison* template in PowerPoint.

2. Students double-click inside the text boxes to add words.

    •   Students can click on the Undo button on the toolbar if they accidentally resize, delete, or move something.

3. Students can add new text boxes if necessary.

    •   To insert a new text box, students go to the Drawing toolbar and click on the Text Box tool. Students drag their mouse on the slide to create the text box. If the Drawing toolbar is not visible, student can go to the View menu, click on Toolbars, and then add a check mark next to Drawing.

4. Students should use a different font color to represent each holiday.

    • To change the font color of a word, students first highlight the word then go to the Formatting toolbar and click on the arrow next to the Font Color button and select the color of their choice.

5. Students insert clip art into the slides. The clip art can then be resized or moved.

    • To insert clip art, students go to the Drawing toolbar and click on the Insert Clip Art button. They enter a descriptive word for the picture they are looking for in the search box and press Search. Students then select a picture from the search results and insert it into the slide either by double-clicking it, or by single-clicking it, then pressing Insert.

    • To resize the picture proportionally, students click on a corner handlebar and, holding down the mouse button, drag it diagonally to the desired size. To move the picture within the slide, students click and hold down the mouse button in the center of the picture and drag it to the desired location.

6. Students save their presentation.

7. Students print their slide show by going to the File menu and clicking on Print > Print What > Slides > OK.

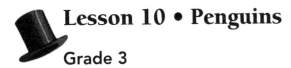

Lesson 10 • Penguins

Grade 3

Lesson Description

The class brainstorms what they know about penguins. The teacher reads aloud an article in a children's wildlife magazine, *Ranger Rick*, and the students take notes as a way to gather information. Students, working in groups of two or three, then formulate five questions about penguins that they will research online.

Students write up the questions in the *Penguins* template, which prompts them to formulate a question for each slide and then answer it. Students are encouraged to focus on quality questions and answers, since they might otherwise choose to answer with minimal writing or use only pictures. Further, students are instructed to give detailed, accurate answers. In this exercise they are not allowed to ask "yes or no" questions, or questions that can be answered in a single word.

Students take on the role of teaching other students when they share their questions and insights. For example, the question, "What other animal also goes back to the same place each year to breed?" would allow students to share their knowledge of salmon with classmates.

Students then brainstorm where they can find answers to their questions. They may suggest using library books, online resources, or videos like *March of the Penguins*. The last slide in the *Penguins* template provides links to pre-selected online resources for students to follow. As students read online information, they add two more questions to their penguin booklets.

After writing the selected questions in their own words and illustrating the slides with photographs and clip art, students check spelling and examine sentence structure. Students learn to acknowledge resources, which are listed for them on the References slide.

After completing this research project, students print the slides as handouts, then cut out the pages and staple them together into a booklet.

Students then use the *Comparing Penguins* template to complete a Venn diagram to compare penguins to other birds (Fig. 10.1). This may be done first as a class activity. Students choose the bird they prefer and write a sentence saying why they prefer it under the diagram.

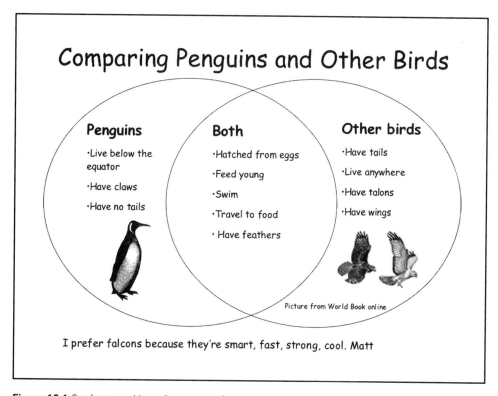

Figure 10.1 Students use Venn diagrams to demonstrate comparisons.

Assessment

Students complete the *Penguins Evaluation* checklist to help guide them as they do their research, and to help them stay focused on the required task. The checklist is provided on the CD as an Excel document that can be modified by the teacher.

Higher Order Thinking Skills	Computer Skills Practiced	Subject Areas and Standards Addressed
Application: Students discover new information, understand, and summarize. **Analysis:** Students analyze information, and select appropriate information to explain the answers to their questions. **Synthesis:** Students invent questions for research. **Evaluation:** Students evaluate what they have learned, and compare penguins with other birds.	Enter information in Outline pane, details in Slide view Page up, Page down Navigate online Move between browser window and PowerPoint window Add or remove bullets Right-click a Web link to open the page in a browser window Copy pictures from Web sites and paste them onto PowerPoint slides Print the slide show as handouts, or as slides	NETS•S: 1.a, 3.a, b, c English Language Arts: NL-ENG.K-12.7, .8 Science: NS.K-4.3 LIFE SCIENCE

Resources Needed

Journals

Ranger Rick Magazine, January 2006, National Wildlife Federation

Web sites

Food Chain of the Emperor Penguin: http://warrensburg.k12.mo.us/Webquest/penguins/

PBS, The World of Penguins: www.pbs.org/wnet/nature/penguins/

Sea World Animals (search for penguins): www.seaworld.org/Search/query.htm

Time for Kids, interview with Luc Jacquet, Director, *March of the Penguins*: www.timeforkids.com/TFK/news/story/0,6260,1097175,00.html

Online encyclopedia; World Book online encyclopedia is recommended (www.worldbookonline.com)

Zoom Birds, Enchanted Learning: www.enchantedlearning.com/subjects/birds/

PowerPoint Activity

1. Students open the *Penguins* template in PowerPoint.

2. Students work in Outline view to enter questions.

3. Students answer the questions, working in Slide view. Students search for answers at Web sites listed on the Resources slide, using PowerPoint and the browser at the same time. Students also copy pictures to insert into their slide show (Fig. 10.2).

    - To open a Web site, students right-click the link on the Resources slide then left click on Open. Internet Explorer will automatically open to the assigned Web address.

    - To return to their slide show, students go to the Taskbar and click on PowerPoint.

    - To copy a picture from a Web site, students right-click the picture, then left-click on Copy. They return to their slide show and right-click on a blank spot on the slide, then left-click on Paste.

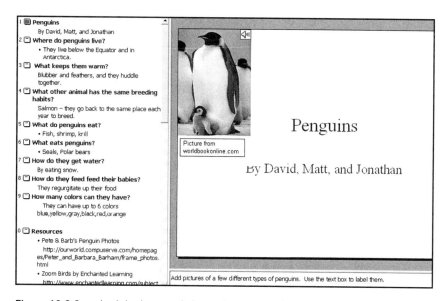

Figure 10.2 Sample slide show made by students researching penguins

5. Students complete Slides 1–8 on the template, then save the slide show.

6. Student print their slide show by going to the File menu and clicking on Print > Print What > Handouts. Students select the number of slides then click on OK.

7. Students open the *Penguin Comparison* template.

8. Students enter text describing the comparison, resizing text as necessary.

   • To resize text, students first highlight the text they want to change then go to the Formatting toolbar and click on the large A button to enlarge it or the small A button to make it smaller.

9. Students insert pictures of a penguin and another type of bird. These pictures can come from the Clip Gallery, Microsoft Office Online Clip Art, or from an online encyclopedia.

10. Students save the presentation.

11. Student print their slide show by going to the File menu and clicking on Print > Print What > Slides > OK.

Extensions and Modifications

Students conduct research on any given topic, by brainstorming, reading an interesting article about the subject, and then formulating questions on a given topic. The teacher modifies the *Penguins* template according to the topic and students use the research template to write up and answer their questions. The teacher also helps students find relevant, age-appropriate online resources. Instructions can be written in Notes View.

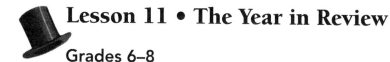

Lesson 11 • The Year in Review

Grades 6–8

Lesson Description

At the end of the school year, students reflect on events that took place throughout the year. They visit pre-selected news Web sites, and in groups they review events that occurred on the global, national, local, school, and personal level. Students list these events on a timeline, and then make a collage with pictures and photographs of these events using images copied from news Web sites that depict historical events. Students also include materials that show some significant events that occurred at school, as well as photographs of themselves on a field trip or doing a particular activity.

The *Year in Review* template provides graphic organizers for brainstorming events of the year (Fig. 11.1), and placing them on a timeline. It then presents prompts for writing about those events in a personal way. Students can select the prompts that inspire them and delete extra slides. Students write a sentence to identify the most interesting, the funniest, the most important, and the best or worst thing that happened to them during the year. Older students first complete the template to brainstorm ideas, and then select one significant event from which to write a detailed descriptive paragraph.

Students then collect pictures from the Internet and paste them onto the first slide of the template to make a collage. They also insert photographs of themselves from school or other activities, and draw original pictures and insert them. They print the collage and the timeline, and open a Microsoft Word document and write a descriptive paragraph about the most meaningful event of the school year.

200X – Brainstorm Events				
Global	National	Local	School	Personal

Figure 11.1 At the end of the year, students use the *Year in Review* template to brainstorm events that occurred during the year, finding examples of global, national, local, school, and personal events.

Assessment

Students use the *Year in Review Instructions* sheet and checklist to keep them focused on the work to be done for this assignment. The instruction sheet and checklist is provided on the CD as a Word document that can be modified by the teacher.

Higher Order Thinking Skills	Computer Skills Practiced	Subject Areas and Standards Addressed
Application: Use information to illustrate important events of the year. **Analysis:** Organize events into global, national, local, school, and personal topics; enter them on a timeline. **Synthesis:** Create an original collage to convey ideas; write original ideas to describe personal experiences. **Evaluation:** Assess events and choose the most significant event as it relates to your life; support choices with an explanation.	Insert text Insert, resize, and move clip art and photographs Delete unnecessary slides Print slides two per page	NETS•S: 1.a; 3.b, c English Language Arts: NL-ENG.K-12.4, .8, .12 Visual Arts: NA-VA. K-4.1, .3

Resources Needed

Web sites

National Geographic News for Kids: http://news.nationalgeographic.com/kids/

News By Kids (helps students to make a news report): www.henry.k12.ga.us/pges/instruction/kid-pages/news-team/

Scholastic.com news archives: http://teacher.scholastic.com/scholasticnews/news/archive.asp

Time for Kids: www.timeforkids.com/TFK/

Vanderbilt University, Television Nightly News Archive (scroll down and click on TV-News Search): http://tvnews.vanderbilt.edu/index.pl?SID=20060419804748535&UID=&CID=&auth=&code=

Washington Post for Kids (scroll down and click on More News):
www.washingtonpost.com/wp-srv/kidspost/orbit/kidspost.html

Miscellaneous

Save newspapers or record TV news broadcasts from December 31st of the previous year; these provide excellent summaries of events.

Hard copies of magazines for kids that provide news, i.e., *Time for Kids*

PowerPoint Activity

1. Students open the *Year in Review* template in PowerPoint (Fig. 11.2).

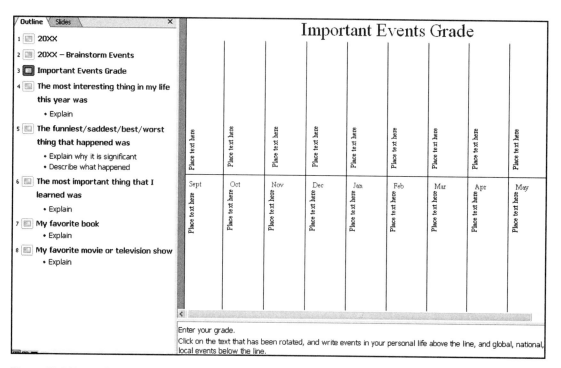

Figure 11.2 *Year in Review* template

2. Students scroll down to Slide 2 and enter important events on the timeline. Students click on a text box above the line to enter personal events, or on a text box below the line to enter global, national, local, and school events. Students should save their slide show often when working on this activity.

3. On Slide 1, students create a collage of images that illustrate the events of the year. To start, students open Internet Explorer and visit Time for Kids online to find a picture of an important event that took place over the course of the year. They may also visit other Web sites to find pictures of their favorite book or movie of the year.

4. Students copy pictures from these Web sites and paste them in their slide show to add to their collage.

- To copy pictures from a Web site, students right-click the picture they want to copy, click on Copy, then click on Year in Review in the Taskbar to open PowerPoint. In Slide view in PowerPoint students click where they want to put the picture, right-click, and then click on Paste.

5. Students create an original picture to add to the collage using a drawing program such as Kid Pix, Microsoft Paint, or AppleWorks Paint.

   - To copy their picture from Microsoft Paint, students click on the Selection tool (which can be described as "marching ants") and drag the mouse over the picture. They then go to the Edit menu and click on Copy. Students click on Year in Review in the Taskbar to go back to PowerPoint, then right-click where they want to place the picture, and left click on Paste.

6. Students insert photographs of school events or of themselves on field trips or doing activities at school into the collage. If students don't have pictures for a certain event, they can use clip art. Once all pictures have been added, they can be moved, resized, and layered to complete the collage.

   - To insert a photograph, students go to the Insert menu and click on Picture > From File. They must browse to find the picture where it is saved, possibly on a removable drive, a network, or in My Documents. They can either double-click the file or click on Insert to place the picture on the slide.

   - To insert clip art, students go to the Drawing toolbar and click on the Insert Clip Art button. They enter a descriptive word for the picture they are looking for in the search box and press Search. Students then select a picture from the search results and insert it into the slide either by double-clicking it, or by single-clicking it, then pressing Insert.

   - To resize the picture proportionally, students click on a corner handlebar and, holding down the mouse button, drag it diagonally to the desired size. To move the picture within the slide, students click and hold down the mouse button in the center of the picture and drag it to the desired location.

7. Students follow the prompts on the remaining slides to enter information about the year's events.

8. Students delete unnecessary slides by clicking on them in Outline View and pressing the Delete key.

9. Student print full-page slides for Slides 1 and 2 by going to the File menu and clicking on Print > Slides > Print Range > (type in 1-2) > OK.

10. Students look at their collage, timeline, and slide show and then select the most meaningful event for them for the year. Students then open a Microsoft Word document and write a descriptive paragraph about that event.

Extensions and Modifications

- Younger students complete a similar Year in Review assignment using a projection device. The teacher explores an online news Web site with the class, and students suggest important events of the year. Students then discuss the meaning of a global, a national, and a local event. Together, the teacher and students enter important events on the timeline, underneath the line. Photographs that were taken during the school year are projected onto the large screen, and students share some of the important events that happened in their personal lives during the year.

  Students complete the timeline at computer stations alone or with a partner. Above the line, they write in a word, phrase, or sentence to identify the events. They enter the year on the first page, and with adult help they insert photographs of themselves that have been taken during the school year. They may choose a couple of events to write sentences about, deleting unnecessary slides by clicking on them in Outline view and then pressing the Delete key. Students print the remaining slides, one per page, and add drawings on the hard copy to represent events that took place. They may choose to label their drawings.

- Using suggestions outlined at the News for Kids Web site, students form groups of three and create a news report about an important news event of the past year. Students can take on the roles of news anchor/script writer, reporter/researcher, or cameraman/picture and photo finder. They create a PowerPoint slide show with pictures, write a script, and then the announcer reads the news to the class while the slide show is projected on a large screen.

Lesson 12 • Internet Research 101

Grades 7, 8

Lesson Description

As students conduct research, they need to learn how to find resources that are relevant and valid. Teachers should begin this lesson with a discussion that reviews what students already know about searching the Internet and about how search engines work. The teacher may need to point out that the Web is a self-publishing medium, which is not always reliable, and that there are different ways to find information on the Internet.

Students form small groups and use the *Search Techniques* template to guide them through the activity. Students summarize the University of Albany's Checklist of Internet Research Tips and answer the questions about search techniques that are found on the template (Fig. 12.1). They explore subject directories such as Yahooligans or Infomine, which are helpful for finding resources that are recommended by experts. The last slide invites students to share additional information they learned about searching the Web.

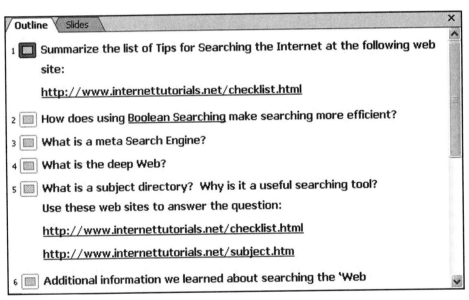

Figure 12.1 Students use the *Search Techniques* template to summarize information they read online about searching for information on the Internet.

After completing the group assignment, student researchers work on their own to apply the search techniques on a given topic, using the *References* template (Fig. 12.2) as a guide.

Students explore what they already know about the topic with the KWHL chart graphic organizer included in the template. They use a directory (a search engine where they enter their question in plain English), a metasearch engine, an online Encyclopedia, and picture sources to find resources for information about their topic. Using the Record of Online Searching table in the template, they document the paths they took to find online resources. They list the URL where they began the search, the keywords or path they followed, and two useful resources that they found. Students then find at least two print resources in the school library, and compare the information and its source. Finally, students generate a bibliography of the online and print resources they will use for a research project on the topic. Students can print their slide show and then use the resources they have found to complete the research project.

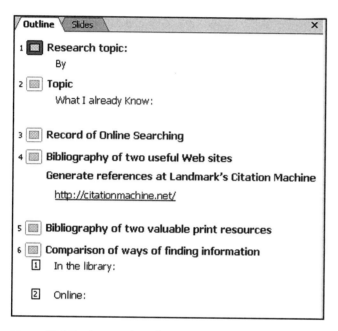

Figure 12.2 Students work on their own to search for information using the *References* template (shown in the Outline pane) to help structure the activity.

It's important to teach students to use their own words and to avoid unethical plagiarism. The teacher points out the Web page title (on the title bar at the top of the window), the author's name and information (often listed at the bottom of the page), and the URL or Web address in the address bar. Students note that all of the publishing information is often not provided on a Web page, as it is in a book.

Assessment

Students complete the *Internet Research* checklist to help guide them in this activity. The checklist is provided on the CD as an Excel document that can be modified by the teacher.

Higher Order Thinking Skills	Computer Skills Practiced	Subject Areas and Standards Addressed
Analysis: To answer the given questions, students analyze information and compare the value of Internet research and research conducted in a library **Synthesis:** Students identify what they already know about Internet searching; they explore new ideas and synthesize information about new ways of doing research. They apply the new techniques they have learned to locate resources **Evaluation:** Students evaluate, summarize, and explain new information	Right-click a hyperlink on a PowerPoint slide to open the Web page Use PowerPoint to make notes from Web pages, keeping a PowerPoint and a Web browser window open at the same time. Resize windows so that both are visible at the same time Use the taskbar to move between two open applications Find the title, author, and URL of a Web page Copy a Web page address and paste it onto a PowerPoint slide Print select slides in a slide show, two per page	NETS•S: 3.a, b, c English Language Arts: NL-ENG.K-12.7, .8

Resources Needed

Landmark's Son of Citation Machine (for generating a bibliography): http://citationmachine.net

University of Albany, New York: Checklist of Internet Research Tips: www.internettutorials.net/checklist.html

Online encyclopedia; World Book online encyclopedia (www.worldbookonline.com) is recommended

PowerPoint Activity

Group Assignment

1. Students open the *Internet Research* template in PowerPoint.

2. Students enter answers to the questions on the slides. Some of the slides contain hyperlinks to the information that they will need.

   • To open a hyperlink, students right-click on a link, click on Hyperlink then Open. This opens Internet Explorer, or the browser installed on the computer, to the designated Web page.

Individual Assignment

1. Students open the *References* template in PowerPoint.

2. Students fill out the KWHL table on Slide 2.

3. Students search for online resources and fill in the Record of Online Searching table on Slide 3. Students use the Tab key to move from cell to cell inside the table. Students will need to switch between the PowerPoint window and the browser window to copy information. They can use the Taskbar to toggle between the two windows or set up their screen to see both windows side-by-side. Students should take care to save their PowerPoint presentation before switching to the Web browser.

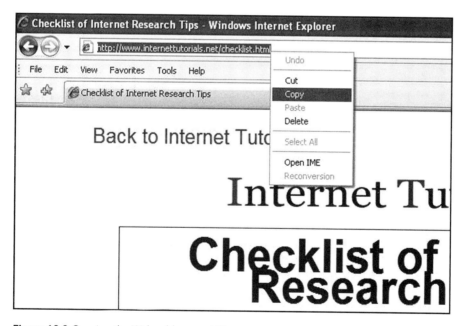

Figure 12.3 Copying the Web address, or URL.

- To view both windows side-by-side, students click on the Restore Down button in the top right corner of the PowerPoint window. This will make the window smaller, and it can be resized by dragging on the window border when the mouse becomes a two-way arrow. Students can move the window by dragging the title bar. Students repeat for the browser window.

- To copy the address of a Web page, students click in the Address bar in the Web browser, highlight the URL, right-click, then click on Copy (Fig. 12.3). They return to PowerPoint, click in the appropriate place, right-click and then click on Paste.

4. After students have found a useful Internet site, they should click on Add to Favorites (found on the browser toolbar) so that they can return to the site easily by accessing their Favorites menu.

5. Students use the Son of Citation Machine Web site to make a bibliography (Fig. 12.4). Students click on MLA or APA to select the format of the reference. They scroll down and select Web Page under Non-Print Resources then complete as much information from the Web page as needed for the bibliography.

Citation Machine: © The Landmark Project. Reprinted with permission.

Figure 12.4 Note the location of "Web Page" on the Son of Citation Machine site.

Once the students have inserted information from a Web site, they click on Submit. Students highlight the reference, right-click and click on Copy, then return to PowerPoint, right-click on the slide, and click on Paste. Students repeat this procedure for other references.

6. Students save and print their slide show when it is complete.

Instruction Writing Lessons
Write to Teach Others

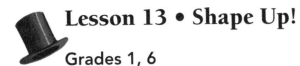

Lesson 13 • Shape Up!

Grades 1, 6

Lesson Description

Upper elementary or middle school students work with younger "buddies" to teach them how to use a digital camera and to help them recognize and record characteristics of different geometric shapes. Working as "technical assistants," older students can help with uploading pictures and printing but allow the younger students to take all of the photographs and to complete the work themselves.

In small groups, younger students take turns using a digital camera to photograph shapes they find in the school building and outside that match the shapes listed on the *Shapes Worksheet*. Younger students may find it difficult to find some of the shapes and may need the older students' assistance. Students use a printed copy of the *Shapes Worksheet* as a checklist to monitor their progress and to help ensure they photograph each of the desired shapes.

First-graders often get a thrill out of using the digital camera and viewing their photographs instantly—on the computer, projected onto a large screen, or on a printed worksheet. Remind them to use the LCD or viewfinder to check that they do not cut off heads in their photos or have their fingers covering the lens (Fig. 13.1).

Figure 13.1 Students learn to use the viewfinder or the LCD panel to compose their photographs.

Students then use the *Shapes* template to label each shape and adjust shape colors, and they get help from older students to insert and resize their photos on the corresponding PowerPoint slides on the template. Using the table provided in the *Shapes* template, students compare shape characteristics, identifying whether they are flat or three-dimensional, have pointed or rounded edges, and so on. When finished, older students help younger students print the *Shapes* template slides to create a booklet of their work (Fig. 13.2). Full-size pages of each shape, highlighting photographs taken by many students, can be displayed in the classroom.

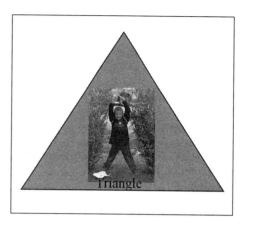

Figure 13.2 Sample pages from shapes booklets. First-graders take the photographs, and then sixth-graders insert the photos into the various shapes.

Assessment

Younger and older students both use the *Shapes* checklist to assess their work upon completion, rating themselves on the assignment criteria. The checklist is provided on the CD as an Excel document that can be modified by the teacher.

Higher Order Thinking Skills	Computer Skills Practiced	Subject Areas and Standards Addressed
Application: Apply knowledge of shapes to identify examples in the environment, examine the requirements on a check-list, and take photographs of real objects that relate to identified shapes	Insert text Change the color of shapes Insert pictures from file (with assistance) Print handouts, three or six per page	NETS•S: 1.a, b; 2.a, b; 3.a Math: NM-GEO.PK-2.1
Analysis: Analyze shapes and compare drawings with what is seen and photographed		
Synthesis: Create and design a booklet on shapes		

Resources Needed

Digital camera

PowerPoint Activity

1. Students open the *Shapes* template in PowerPoint.

2. Students click on Slide 1 in the Slide pane and enter their name.

3. Students click on the Page Down key on the keyboard to get to Slide 2, then label the shape in the text box.

4. Students click on the desired shape to select it, go to the Drawing toolbar and click on the Fill Color button, then select a color.

5. With the shape still selected, students insert the photograph. The picture can then be resized and moved on the slide.

    *   To insert a photograph, they go to the Insert menu and click on Picture > From File. They must browse to find the picture where it is saved, possibly on a removable drive, a network, or in My Documents. They can either double-click the file or click on Insert to place the picture on the slide.

    *   To resize the picture proportionally, students click on a corner handlebar and, holding down the mouse button, drag it diagonally to the desired size. To move the picture within the slide, they click and hold down the mouse button in the center of the picture and drag it to the desired location.

6. Students repeat this process for the other shapes. To add new shapes to the template, students go to the Drawing toolbar and then select Basic Shapes from the AutoShapes Menu.

7. Students click on a slide in the Outline pane, then press the Delete button on the keyboard to delete any slides they don't want.

8. Students complete the Shapes Comparison table on Slide 11 (Fig 13.3). Students place an x or a number in a cell to compare the characteristics of shapes.

Shape	Flat	3D	Pointed edges	Rounded edges	# of sides
(circle)					
(ellipse)					
(square)					
(rectangle)					
(triangle)					
(diamond)					
(cylinder)					
(cube)					
(heart)					

Figure 13.3 Students compare shapes on the Shapes Comparison table, noting whether they are three-dimensional or flat, whether their edges are pointed or flat, and the number of sides.

9. Students print their slides by going to the File menu and clicking on Print> Print What > Handouts > 2 slides per page > OK. *Note:* To prevent the slide outline from printing, the mark next to Frame Slides must be unchecked.

Extensions and Modifications

- Have younger students take photographs on their own, but not make PowerPoint slide shows. The older buddy, a teacher, or a parent volunteer inserts the pictures for the younger students and prints them as handouts, three per page. The slides should include note lines on the side of each photo. Younger students then write next to each picture to identify the shape; who is in the picture; or where the subject is located. Staple the pages together to make a class booklet of shapes; allow children to take turns sharing the booklet with their families.

- Have students draw their own shapes picture on the computer (Fig. 13.4). To make this task easier for students, save the shapes on the template. The students' job is to duplicate a shape. They will click on the shape to select it by holding down the CTRL key and then pushing down the D key once. Students can then resize, recolor, or move the shape. To move it, they use the arrow keys on the keyboard or the mouse. Some students may even be able to rotate a shape, using the Rotate button on the Drawing Menu. Students then count how many of each shape they have used and give their picture a title. The idea for this lesson was inspired by a shapes drawing assignment by Anne Hayes, a teacher at St. Luke School.

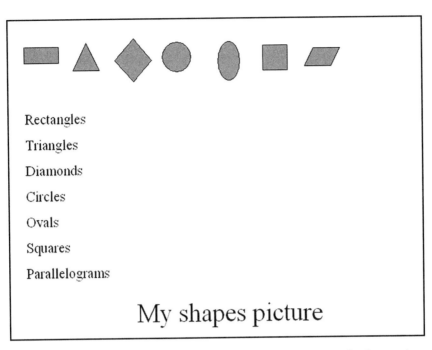

Rectangles

Triangles

Diamonds

Circles

Ovals

Squares

Parallelograms

My shapes picture

Figure 13.4 Shapes have been inserted on this slide on the template so that first-graders can drag, resize, duplicate, and recolor them to make a picture.

Lesson 14 • A Day at the Gallery

Grade 5

Lesson Description

Students research a topic to prepare for a field trip to an art museum. Before the field trip, students form groups, and each group chooses a theme to explore while they are at the museum. They then conduct research about their theme using online and print resources from the museum as well as other resources. During the outing, students gather information and take photographs of artwork to include in a presentation. Instead of just touring the museum and listening to a commentary, this lesson allows students to really engage with the art as they select works that illustrate their chosen theme. Later, students will use PowerPoint to share their photographs and themes with other students.

Successful topics for fifth-graders have included:

- Realistic versus abstract art

- Art that inspires questions

- The use of colors, shapes, and imagination in paintings

- The color wheel and the primary, secondary, and tertiary colors

- Warm colors versus cool colors

- The symbolic meaning of colors (e.g., Red suggests love and passion.)

Before visiting your chosen museum, call ahead to make sure photography is allowed. Many museums allow photography as long as no flash is used. Have students practice using their digital cameras ahead of time so they understand how to turn off the flash. When you contact the museum, you might also ask if a docent would be available during your visit to help point out art works that fit your students' chosen themes. Remind students of proper museum etiquette ahead of time.

Even if the museum allows photography, there are still limits on what you may do with photographs of the displayed art. If you plan to use the photographs only in educational presentations within the classroom, that will likely qualify as Fair Use. Other uses may be restricted by copyright law. One time, my students wanted to enter their museum slide shows in a multimedia competition but were unable to due to copyright restrictions on the artwork.

During the field trip, students can have fun personalizing their photographs by taking pictures of each other standing next to their chosen works of art. Students should also note the title and artist of each piece of art they photograph so that they can acknowledge the source in the References slide they will later create.

Assessment

Students can use the *Art Gallery Field Trip* checklist to help guide them in this activity. The checklist is provided on the accompanying CD as an Excel document that can be modified by the teacher.

Higher Order Thinking Skills	Computer Skills Practiced	Subject Areas and Standards Addressed
Application: Apply knowledge of an identified topic; discover evidence in artwork, present to an audience **Analysis:** Analyze artwork and infer meaning **Synthesis:** Arrange photographs and design a meaningful presentation	Use a digital camera; zoom, turn off the flash Upload pictures from a digital camera to a computer Insert text and photographs on slides Resize photographs Crop photographs Modify photograph's brightness level	NETS•S: 1.a, b; 2.a, b, d; 3.a, b, c Visual Arts: NA-VA.K-4.2 English Language Arts: NL-ENG.K-12.12

Resources Needed

One digital camera per group

Additional Resources

Color Matters—Design Art: www.colormatters.com/colortheory.html

Wassily Kandinsky claimed that when he saw color he heard music: www.ibiblio.org/wm/paint/auth/kandinsky/

Sanford Art: A Lifetime of Color: www.alifetimeofcolor.com/study/g_color.html

About.com—Color Symbolism: Webdesign.about.com/od/color/a/aa072604.htm

Design with Color—Color symbolism (scroll down the page): www.devx.com/projectcool/Article/19987/0/page/3

PowerPoint Activity

1. Students open a new blank presentation in PowerPoint and choose the Title Only slide layout.

2. Students plan the content of the slide show by writing a title or a question for each slide in the Outline pane.

3. Students add a background to their slides (Fig. 14.2).

- To add the same background to all the slides, students right-click on the slide and then click on Background. They select the color and the fill effect then click on Apply to All. To change the background for one slide, they select a color and Fill and then click on Apply. To remove the background from a particular slide, they right-click the slide, click on Background and check Omit Background Graphics from Master, then click Apply.

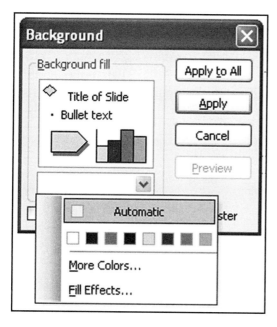

Figure 14.2 Select a color for the background of the slide and apply it to the current slide or to all slides in the slide show.

4. Students insert a photograph into their slide show. The photograph can be resized, cropped, and brightened.

- To insert a photograph, students go to the Insert menu and click on Picture > From File to place a photograph on the slide. To move the picture within the slide, students click and hold down the mouse button in the center of the picture and drag it to the desired location.

- Students may resize the picture by clicking on it to highlight it and then clicking on a corner handlebar and dragging. To resize the image proportionally (so that it doesn't look "stretched" or "squished"), students can click on a corner handlebar and, holding down the shift key, drag the handlebar to the desired size.

- To crop a picture, students can click on the picture to select it, then click on the Crop tool on the Picture toolbar. They then drag a handlebar to crop the picture.

- To brighten or darken an image, students click on the image to select it, then click on More Brightness or Less Brightness on the Picture toolbar until they are satisfied with how the picture looks.

5. Students create a References slide listing the titles of the featured artwork and names of the artists. The museum they visited should receive credit as well. This should be the final slide in the presentation.

Extensions and Modifications

- Similar projects can be designed for students visiting history or science museums, or for other types of field trips such as visits to a zoo or fire station.

- A follow-up activity to the art museum field trip involves students writing a story about their favorite piece of art or creating similar artwork. During one visit to a museum, there was an exhibition of portraits of Mao Tse Tung by Andy Warhol, which fascinated the students. Taking digital photographs of themselves, the students inserted and resized one picture on a PowerPoint slide, and then duplicated it at least nine times on the slide. Then they printed the slide in gray scale and, using a marker to add color, they made Andy Warhol–style posters.

Lesson 15 • Presidents Day

Grades 1, 8

Lesson Description

Older students use the *Presidents Day* template, which includes Web resources, and the *Presidents Day Instructions* sheet to create an interactive slide show about U.S. presidents to present to younger students on Presidents Day. The slide shows include information about past presidents, presidential monuments, and presidents on U.S. coins. They also include information about our current president, including family, pets, and home. Older students work with younger "buddies" to help navigate Web sites to collect information about U.S. presidents and copy, paste, and format pictures and text on individual slides. The older students make the slideshow interactive by creating presidential quiz questions and inserting hyperlinks to the last two "Correct!" and "Try again!" slides on the template that will give the younger students feedback about the answers they select. The "Correct!" and "Try again!" template slides have an action button that, when clicked on, will take the viewer back to the previously viewed slide, making the slide show easy to navigate.

Younger students also learn technology skills while they create pictures in a drawing program such as Kid Pix or Microsoft Paint in response to one or more questions in the slide show, or select online images and clip art. The pictures created in the drawing program are then pasted into slides in the Presidents Day slide show by older students. When finished, the slides can be printed and stapled together by older students to create a booklet for the younger students.

Assessment

Students use the *Presidents Day Instructions* sheet as a checklist to ensure they include a variety of presidential facts based on the criteria listed, and to help keep track of the assignment requirements, including inserting at least two slides made by the younger buddy, adding pictures, creating a references slide, including an open-ended question, and making sure wording and the information presented is appropriate for younger students. This instruction sheet is provided on the CD as an Excel document that can be modified by the teacher.

Higher Order Thinking Skills	Computer Skills Practiced	Subject Areas and Standards Addressed
Analysis: Analyze information **Synthesis:** Organize information and arrange slides with interactive links; create an original product to explain the U.S. presidency to first grade students **Evaluation:** Select age-appropriate material	Insert text and graphics on slides Insert action buttons or hyperlinks, and back buttons to previously viewed slides Copy and paste URLs Copy graphics drawn in a paint program and paste them into PowerPoint Move between different PowerPoint views	NETS•S: 1.a, b; 2.a, b; 3.a, b, c; 5.b English Language Arts: NL-ENG.K-12.4, 5, 6, 8, 12 Social Studies: NSS-C.5-8.3

Resources Needed

Web sites

American Presidents: Life Portraits: www.americanpresidents.org

Grolier Online: http://ap.grolier.com/browse?type=profiles#pres

PBS President for a Day: http://pbskids.org/democracy/presforaday/

The White House: www.whitehouse.gov

The White House for kids: www.whitehouse.gov/kids/

U.S. Coins at Enchanted Learning: www.enchantedlearning.com/econ/Coins.shtml

Software

Drawing software such as Kid Pix, Microsoft Paint, or Appleworks Paint

Miscellaneous

Coins

PowerPoint Activity

1. Students open the *Presidents Day* template in PowerPoint.

2. Older students and their younger buddies visit the Web sites listed on the Resources slide together and gather information about the U.S. presidency.

   • To open the links on the Resources slide, students right-click on a Web address, and in the pop-up menu move the mouse over Hyperlink, and click on Open.

3. Students create quiz questions based on the six criteria listed on the *Presidents Day Instructions* sheet and type the questions into the PowerPoint template slides, adding relevant images and clip art, copying and pasting source URLs under images taken from Web sites (Fig. 15.1). Web site source URLs are then added to the Resources slide, if not already there.

   • To copy and paste pictures from Web pages, students right-click the picture, click on Copy, return to the slide show, click on the appropriate slide, and then click on Paste.

4. Students provide two possible answers to each quiz question (one true, one false) on each slide. Each answer should be made into a hyperlink that links to either the the Correct! or Try again! slide within the template. Hyperlinks will only work when in Slide Show view, and hyperlinked text will appear in gray unless a different font color is selected.

   • To insert a hyperlink, students right-click the text or image representing the answer, then click on Hyperlink. Under Link To, they select Place in This Document, highlight appropriate response slide, and then click OK.

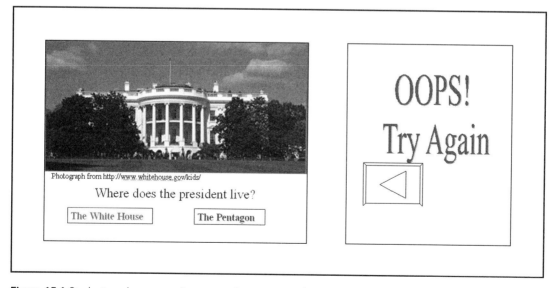

Figure 15.1 Students make up questions to teach younger students about U.S. presidents. The picture on the right shows the slide that a user reaches if they click on the wrong answer in the slide show.

5. Older students write at least one open-ended question, such as "What would you like best about being president?" and add the text to a blank PowerPoint slide in the template. Younger buddies then create images and/or text to answer the open-ended question. Samples of slides made by younger students are shown in Figure 15.2.

6. Older students work with younger buddies to help resize images as needed, save the file, and then paste the images on the corresponding question slides in the PowerPoint template.

7. Students save the slide show, then print the slide show with two slides per page by goint to the File Menu and clicking on Print > Print What > Handouts > 2 slides per page > OK.

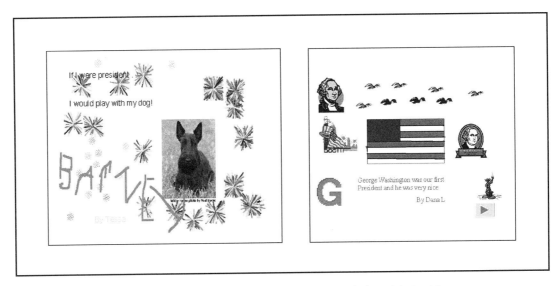

Figure 15.2 Sample slides made by younger students in collaboration with their older buddies.

Extensions and Modifications

Students who experience problems inserting and formatting hyperlinks can omit the last two slides. Their slide show will not be interactive.

If students would like to add their own action buttons, they can click on the Slide Show menu, click on Action buttons, click on the button of choice, and then drag the mouse from corner to corner to insert the button.

Students might use their knowledge of interactive slide shows to make an interactive storybook with two or more possible endings.

Lesson 16 • Clay Animation 101

Grades 4–8

Lesson Description

This lesson was inspired by a session given by Adam Van Overmeer, Iowa-Grant School District, at the Governor of Wisconsin's Technology Conference in 2003.

For this project several class sessions (at least six) are required. The results are a fun clay animation made up of 50 PowerPoint slides.

First, students view and evaluate clay animation technique and clay animations made by others. They then form groups of two or three and brainstorm a storyline, including characters, a setting, and a short plot. Figures are created using clay and tinfoil-covered pipe cleaners. Backdrops and props are made from cardboard boxes and construction paper.

Next, students photograph the action in a series of 50 photographs. They insert these pictures into a slide show. This creative assignment sparks their imagination, and there is great excitement when they share their clay animations. The final step is creating step-by-step instructions so that other students may produce a similar project.

How Does Clay Animation Work?

Explore how showing successive images of figures, with small changes in each image, animates the figures, making it seem like they're moving. A flip-book is a very simple example of this technique. Then lead a discussion of commercial clay animations such as *Wallace and Gromit*. Students can view a short excerpt on DVD and explore *Wallace and Gromit* online. Have them read the Interesting Facts section on the Web site. They will discover that it took a production crew of 250 people five years to make the film, and that 24 frames *per second* were used to get the detailed effects. Students will soon understand that they do not have the equipment or the time to perfect their clay animations to this degree, but they can nonetheless explore the creative possibilities of clay animation.

Form Groups, Brainstorm, and Plan

Have students form groups of two or three and brainstorm their plot, setting, and characters. Stress that their plotlines need to be quite short, and as they settle on plots, check their ideas and offer guidance if the story is too long or complicated. Students should be discouraged from recreating TV or movie characters. Instead, encourage students to create original characters: human, animal, or even invented creatures. You may want to discourage plots involving fighting, explosions, and other kinds of violence. Students can browse children's books for ideas and view sample clay animations at the Clay Animation Station (library.thinkquest.org/22316/home. html) and the Clay and Stop-Motion Animation How-To Page (www.animateclay. com). Visit these sites yourself to screen samples for appropriateness before sending your students there. Discuss with students what made the sample clay animations work, what could be improved, what the characters were made of, and what was used for a backdrop.

Using the *Clay Animation Planning Sheet*, students decide on a story. For example, as the following figures illustrate, Griphon and Gary are playing on the playground, ignoring a third child who is crying and wants to play with them. The excluded child cries. (Tears are simulated using small circles of blue clay that move down his face in successive photographs.) In the end, Griphon and Gary ask the third child to join them, and the three of them chase each other around. This is a good example of a plot that is manageable in 50 slides.

Figure 16.1 This clay figure "cries"—small blue circles of clay simulating tears appear to move down his face in successive slides.

Figure 16.2 The clay characters play together on the playground.

Creating Characters, Backdrops, and Props

Now it's time to get out the clay, pipe cleaners, and tinfoil! Students should make two- or three-inch characters using a pipe cleaner covered in tin foil as the skeleton (this method gives figures some flexibility). Students then cover the skeleton in modeling clay, beginning with one color and then accenting with other colors. I've found that younger students tend to make their characters flat, and they need encouragement to explore three-dimensional shapes like spheres, cylinders, and cubes. They learn quickly that the "feet" of their clay figure have to be three-dimensional in order for it to stand without assistance.

Students make backdrops by decorating a cardboard box with colored construction paper, cut-out shapes, and drawings. They should use contrasting colors for the clay figures and the backdrop so that their figures stand out against the surroundings. The box should be at least 18 inches high and 18 inches wide so the edges don't show when photographed. This makes the scene more realistic. The box lids should be cut off to make it easier for students to create their setting.

Students add interest to their backdrop by including props like windows, curtains, and pictures for an indoor scene. Students should be encouraged to consider imaginative uses of color and to come up with creative ideas for backdrops. One group of students made an urban basketball court by cutting out and pasting up a picture of a city skyline (Fig. 16.3). Another group chose the circus as the setting, pulling up a curtain to reveal an audience drawn by the young artists (Fig. 16.4).

Figure 16.3 A photograph of a city skyline creates an urban backdrop.

Figure 16.4 A circus scene.

It's Time to Take Pictures

Now students have their plot planned out and have created all the characters, backdrops, and props they'll need. It's time to start taking pictures! Explain to students that to successfully create the illusion of movement, it is imperative to keep the camera and the backdrop still while moving the clay figures slightly for each photograph. Have students place the camera on a student desk or a tripod, facing the box. Use a flash to ensure even lighting. (It's not a bad idea to have extra batteries on hand in case all the flash photos drain some of the cameras.)

Remind students not to put their fingers in front of the lens or in any of their pictures. Students may need to find innovative ways to support or move their clay figures. In one clay animation, students wanted to create the illusion of basketball players passing the ball and shooting at the goal. They moved the ball through the air by suspending it with fishing line (Fig. 16.5).

Figure 16.5 The basketball is suspended from fishing line.

Finishing Up

If students want to show characters talking, they will be able to insert speech bubbles in PowerPoint at the appropriate moments. Students should aim to complete their storyline in about 50 photographs. Now it's time to add the photographs to a PowerPoint slide show and bring the clay animation to life! Please see the PowerPoint Activity section for detailed information on creating the slide show. Then, the final step in the project will be to have students write detailed instructions so other students can recreate the project. The *Clay Animation Writing Checklist* will help them write the instructions.

Assessment

Students complete the *Clay Animation Planning Sheet* to help guide them in this activity. Students use the *Clay Animation Writing Checklist* to help them write out instructions for duplicating their project. This checklist can also be used for grading. The checklists are provided on the accompanying CD as Excel documents that can be modified by the teacher.

Higher Order Thinking Skills	Computer Skills Practiced	Subject Areas and Standards Addressed
Application: Experiment to get desired animation effects; solve problems that may arise **Analysis:** Analyze the steps and organize a sequence of events to create an impression of movement; organize the photographs in sequence **Synthesis:** Plan, design, and create characters and backdrop	Take photographs with a digital camera and upload them to a computer Insert photographs into PowerPoint slides Insert speech bubbles on a PowerPoint slide Set the timing on the slide show	NETS•S: 1.a, b; 2.a, b, d; 4.b; 6.b Visual Arts: NA-VA.5-8.1, 3 English Language Arts: NL-ENG.K-12.5, 12

Resources Needed

Web sites:

Clay and Stop-Motion Animation How-To Page: www.animateclay.com

Clay Animation Station: library.thinkquest.org/22316/home.html

Wallace and Gromit: www.wallaceandgromit.com

Miscellaneous:

One digital camera per group

Extra batteries

Pipe cleaners, scissors, cardboard boxes, tin foil, construction paper, modeling clay, markers

PowerPoint Activity

1. Students open a new blank presentation in PowerPoint and choose the Title Slide layout.

2. Students type a title for the animation and add the names of the creators.

3. Students go to the Insert menu and click on New Slide. Students select the Blank Slide layout.

4. Students insert each photograph onto a new blank slide.

    *   To insert a photograph, students go to the Insert menu and click on Picture > From File. They must browse to find the picture where it is saved, possibly on a removable drive, a network, or in My Documents. They can either double-click the file or click on Insert to place the picture on the slide.

    *   If you are using PowerPoint 2003 or later, students can go to the Insert menu and click on Picture > New Photo Album and insert all photographs located in one folder. Students select the pictures they want to insert, and click on Insert. Next to Picture Layout they select Fit to Slide, click on Create, and each photograph is inserted on a new slide and sized to fit the slide.

4. Students insert speech bubbles, which can then be resized. Students can also use the Text tool to add text to the bubble.

    *   To insert a speech bubble, students go to the Drawing toolbar and click on Autoshapes > Callouts. Students choose a speech bubble and drag it onto the photograph. They use the handlebars to resize the speech bubble.

5. Students view the slide show. They go to the View menu, then click on Slide Show. Students can press the space bar to advance from slide to slide. It may be preferable to manually advance the slide show, because students can control the timing more accurately.

    If students prefer to set the timing, they go to the Slide Show menu, then click on Slide Transition. Under Advance Slide, they check Automatically After and select the timing of their choice (I find that 00:01 advances too slowly and 00:00 much too quickly). Students click on Apply to All to apply to all slides.

Extensions and Modifications

Students can make animations using clip art or their own drawings rather than clay figures.

Persuasive Writing Lessons
Communicate to Persuade

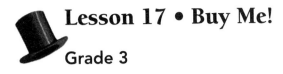

Lesson 17 • Buy Me!

Grade 3

Lesson Description

This lesson was developed with Carole de Young, a colleague and third grade teacher, based on a lesson in the language arts textbook *World of Language* (Silver, Burdett and Ginn, 1996).

Students examine the text of various advertisements to understand the strategies companies use to persuade readers to purchase a product. Students choose an item they would like to advertise. They then brainstorm what information should be included in an ad that will contain no pictures: What will attract the reader's attention? What can be written to highlight the advertised product's features? Students use a checklist and a template to write a persuasive paragraph and use fonts, font colors, WordArt, and white space to create an effective ad.

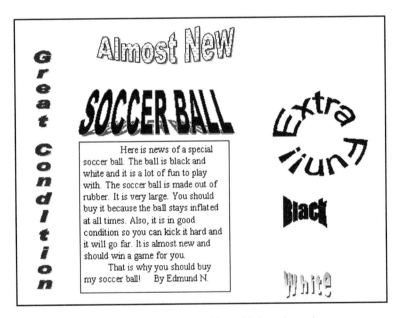

Figure 17.1 Sample advertisement created by a third-grade student.

How Do Ads Use Persuasive Text?

Provide students with online or print advertising that contains large amounts of persuasive text. In groups, have students select two or three ads and brainstorm how the text in the ad tries to persuade the reader to purchase the product. For each ad, have students write down three reasons they find that a person might want to buy the product. Have the groups share their findings with the class.

Individually, have students think of an item or product for which they'd like to create an ad. The item might be something they own or any item or product they're interested in. Students should write a description of the product and three reasons why someone might want to buy it. Remind students to be very descriptive; their ad will contain no images, so their words have to do all the work. Students use the *Buy Me* checklist on the accompanying CD to guide their work.

Create a Persuasive Ad

Now that students have written about their product, it's time to create an eye-catching and persuasive ad. Provide them with the *Why You Should Buy* template from the accompanying CD. Using the template, students place their descriptive text on the slide and use different fonts and font colors, WordArt, and white space to help attract attention and convey their message.

See the PowerPoint Activity section for detailed instructions on creating the PowerPoint ad.

Assessment

Students use the *Buy Me* checklist to help guide their work. The checklist is provided on the accompanying CD as an Excel document that can be modified by the teacher.

Higher Order Thinking Skills	Computer Skills Practiced	Subject Areas and Standards Addressed
Analysis: Analyze the text of advertisements to recognize the strategies advertisers use to persuade readers to purchase a product. **Synthesis:** Design advertisement to convey meaning and attract attention; compose a persuasive paragraph to convince the reader to purchase. **Evaluation:** Recommend a product and support with persuasive reasons to buy the product.	Insert and format text Insert and format WordArt Move and resize text boxes and WordArt	NETS•S: 1.a, b; 2.a, b English Language Arts: NL-ENG.K-12.4, 5 Fine Arts–Visual Arts: NA-VA.K-4.2, 3; NA-VA.5-8.3

Resources Needed

Online or print advertisements (screen for appropriateness)

PowerPoint Activity

1. Students open the *Why You Should Buy* template in PowerPoint.

2. Students click in the text box and enter the text for their ad. They highlight the words they want to replace and type over them.

3. Students go to the Drawing toolbar and then click on the WordArt icon to insert words. They select a WordArt style for the advertisement by clicking on it, then clicking OK.

4. Students enter text and then click OK to place it on the document. Students can move, reshape, and resize WordArt like a graphic.

    •   To move text, students click on it so that it is selected and the handlebars are showing. They hold down the mouse in the middle of the WordArt, and then drag to the desired position. Another option is to use the arrow keys on the keyboard once the text is selected.

    •   To change the shape of the WordArt, students go to the WordArt toolbar and click on the WordArt Shape (Abc) button, then make their selection (Fig. 17.2). To resize, students hold down the mouse on a corner handlebar and drag.

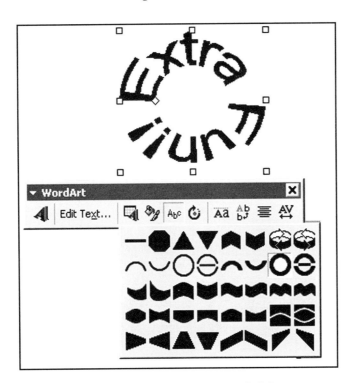

Figure 17.2 When the WordArt has been inserted, click on it to select it, then click on WordArt Shape (Abc) on the WordArt toolbar to modify the shape of the words.

5. Students can also use the WordArt toolbar to make other changes to the WordArt; they can edit, change the color, rotate, adjust the height of letters, align, and change the spacing between characters. Students should be encouraged to experiment with different buttons on the WordArt toolbar.

   • When the students click on WordArt, the WordArt toolbar should show. If it does not, students can go to the View menu and click on Toolbars, then add a checkmark next to WordArt.

6. Students move the text boxes and WordArt on the slide to create a balanced ad with effective use of white space.

Extensions and Modifications

In groups, have students format text from an advertisement you choose. The teacher enters the copy of the ad in plain text on a template and does not show students the original advertisement until they have all completed the project. In this assignment, students will not compose the words, but will focus only on enhancing the meaning of the words. The assignment is to make a full-color, full-page ad.

Each group reads the text together and decides on the intention of the writer and on the most important points in the ad. The ad should grab the reader's attention by emphasizing key words and ideas. Students develop the layout of the page, changing the font, color, and size of the text and adding graphics. They make effective use of white space and use bullets and text alignment. Students also insert appropriate clip art that adds meaning. They are instructed to be selective, to avoid clutter, and to be conscious of adding to the message, not distracting from it. This is a challenging task and can be done by young students, but is generally better suited to middle school students.

Lesson 18 • Persuasive Paragraphs

Grades 5–8

Lesson Description

In my experience, young writers are quick to make judgments and express an opinion. It's typical for many students to arrange ideas in random fashion, jumping from one topic to the next and back again. They need guidance to fully organize and develop their numerous ideas and to back them up with relevant details. This lesson uses PowerPoint as a concept-mapper, helping students to develop their ideas fully and organize them in a coherent fashion in outline form as they compare two objects or ideas and make a judgment about which is better.

Students begin this exercise by brainstorming in groups. This may be done face-to-face or in on an online discussion group. Have students think about two objects or ideas to compare. Ideas might include writing on a computer versus writing on paper, dogs as pets versus fish as pets, visiting the beach versus visiting the mountains, or living in a city versus living in a small town. The teacher should approve the comparison ideas or objects each group chooses.

The *Comparison* template (on the accompanying CD) provides a concept map for students to organize their thoughts about the objects or ideas they will compare. Students think of relevant topics to explore and develop details about each of these topics on subsequent slides. They write an introductory paragraph on the first slide and a concluding paragraph on the last slide. PowerPoint's Outline pane allows students to proceed in nonlinear fashion, jumping from main idea to detail and back and forth between topics as ideas occur to them. Yet they can organize their ideas in coherent fashion under the headings and can add to the introduction and conclusion at any point in the writing process.

Figure 18.1 presents students brainstorming in an online discussion group. In this particular assignment, the topic for discussion was the relative merits of writing on a computer versus writing on paper. Students added new topics as necessary and read and responded to their fellow students' comments.

After brainstorming ideas in groups, students open the *Comparison* template and compare the material (Fig. 18.2). They list items to compare on the first slide of the template.

Writing on a Computer Versus Writing on Paper

Topic 1: Understanding

It might be a little more confusing for someone to learn how to use the computer.

Yeah, but that problem's only with younger kids

Sometimes for adults. My mom…

Topic 2: Getting Information

The computer has lots of information so if you're writing a research paper you can just go on Google and type it in… then you get lots of information that can help you write your paper.

Right, because I hate looking in reference books.

Topic 3: Tools

On computers you can draw and spell check and get a different font so easily.

You can also look words up.

And there's a thesaurus on the computer

Exactly, that is what I was saying.

Topic 4: Organizing

Computers help you organize your writing like on a Web or in charts or graphs

And then you can write an essay on it

Topic 5: Erasing

You can erase on the computer by just pressing a button.

I think it is easier to erase things on the computer instead of erasing on paper.

Yes, and it is also easy because all you have to do is press backspace instead of erasing everything you spell wrong.

Also, if you wrote something on a piece of paper and you noticed it after you wrote more and then you'd have to write the whole part over again because on computer you can add or subtract anything you want with out taking the other part out.

Figure 18.1 Brainstorming session for online discussion group

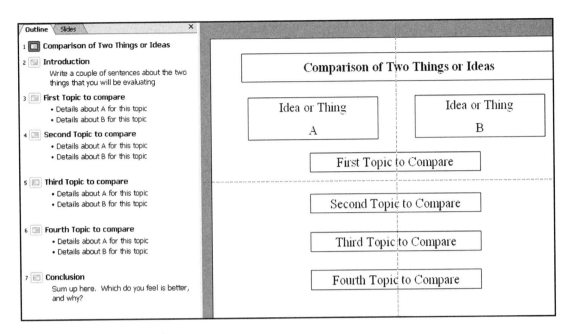

Figure 18.2 *Comparison* template

Students title each of the topics to compare and then add topic details on subsequent slides (remind students to make sure they don't write the same detail twice using different words). Students will initially add details to each topic as bullet points. Have them print the slide show out in Outline form.

Now have students refine their details and place them in a sequence that makes sense. Once that's done, they can begin to craft their persuasive paragraphs right on the slides. Spell Check is available. Setting out details in this fashion helps students ultimately write a convincing final paragraph arguing which idea or item, A or B, is better. You may want to review transition words (e.g., although, in contrast, but, for instance, instead of, also, finally) that may help students construct their persuasive paragraph.

Assessment

Students use the *Persuasive Paragraphs* assessment for the assignment to help them stay on task and complete the steps in the process. They are evaluated for content, including staying on topic, avoiding repetition, and writing meaningful ideas. The *Persuasive Paragraphs* assessment is provided on the accompanying CD as an Excel document that can be modified by the teacher.

Higher Order Thinking Skills	Computer Skills Practiced	Subject Areas and Standards Addressed
Analysis: Students organize their writing as they move from main ideas to details. **Synthesis:** Students rearrange ideas and sentences to convey meaning and avoid repetition. **Evaluation:** Students compare ideas and make decisions based on organized, coherent arguments.	Insert text Navigate from Outline pane to the slide of choice Run Spell Check View slide show Print in Outline format	NETS•S: 1.a, b; 2.a, b English Language Arts: NL-ENG.K-12.4, 5

PowerPoint Activity

1. Students open the *Comparisons* template in PowerPoint in Outline view.

2. Have students click on the Slide pane and click inside the first text box to enter a title for the comparison. Next, students enter their main ideas, for example Writing on a Computer in the "A" text box and Writing on Paper in the "B" text box. From their brainstorming, they enter the topics they will use to compare computer versus paper.

3. Students click on Slide 3 in the Outline pane and enter the first topic to compare in the title bar.

4. Students continue entering topics and begin entering details.

5. Students use the Outline pane to jump between slides as details occur to them.

6. When students have entered all the topics and details they can think of, they print the slide show in Outline View. To do so, they go to the File menu and click on Print > Print What > Outline View > OK. Students may want to click on Preview to check that they have chosen to print in the correct format.

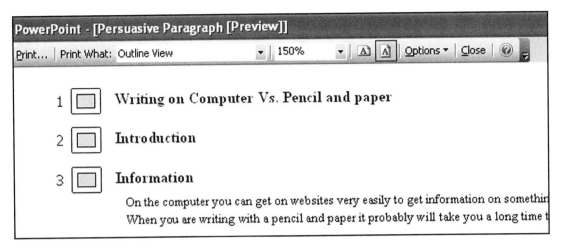

Figure 18.3 Students print their slide shows in Outline view.

7. Students refine their details and place them in a sequence that makes sense. Once that's done, they can begin to craft their persuasive paragraphs right on the slides.

8. Students check their spelling by clicking on the Spell Check icon or by going to the Tools menu and clicking on Spelling.

9. Students save the slide show.

10. Students view the slide show by clicking on the Slide Show icon on the toolbar or by going to the Slide Show menu and clicking on View Show.

Extensions and Modifications

• This template/lesson may be used for comparing other, more advanced topics like industrialized and developing countries. The possibilities are endless.

• Have students send their slides to Microsoft Word (they go to the File menu and click Send To > Microsoft Word), where they finish revising their writing. This extension assumes that students are familiar with editing a Word document. Word has grammar-checking capability and a built-in thesaurus.

Poetic Composition Lessons
Communication with Poetry and Imagery

Lesson 19 • First Rhymes

Grade 1

Lesson Description

Students have fun reading nursery rhymes such as "Humpty Dumpty," "Head, Shoulders, Knees and Toes," "Hey Diddle Diddle," "I'm a Little Teapot," "Ten Little Monkeys," and "One Two Buckle My Shoe." Illustrated versions of these rhymes are available on the Enchanted Learning Web site (www.enchantedlearning.com), and they can be used for this lesson with the Web page projected on a large screen. The rebus pictures help students read difficult words. Have students read each nursery rhyme aloud then identify pairs of rhyming words. Then read them short excerpts from rhyming storybooks they are familiar with, such as Dr. Seuss books, and identify more rhyming words as a class.

Figure 19.1 First graders identify rhymes from familiar verse and from stories they have read.

The *Rhyming Words* template provides slides with common nursery rhymes. Students work alone or in pairs to read the nursery rhymes, highlight and change the font color of rhyming words, and then illustrate each rhyme with clip art to help make connections between words and their meanings (Fig. 19.1). The template also includes slides for students to come up with their own list of words that rhyme with a given word (Fig. 19.2). Finally, a blank slide is provided for poets to make up their own rhyming verse.

Figure 19.2 Students come up with words that rhyme with another given word.

Assessment

Students use the *Rhyming Words* checklist to help guide them in this activity. The checklist is provided on the CD as an Excel document that can be modified by the teacher.

Higher Order Thinking Skills	Computer Skills Practiced	Subject Areas and Standards Addressed
Comprehension: Students understand rhyming and the concept of a rhyme. **Analysis:** Students analyze nursery rhymes, identifying rhyming words. **Synthesis:** Students create original rhymes.	Use Page Down to move to the next slide Highlight text; change font color Use the Undo button on the Standard toolbar Insert text Insert pictures; resize and move pictures	NETS•S: 1.a, b; 2.b English Language Arts: NL-ENG.K-12.6, 12

Resources Needed

Enchanted Learning, rebus rhymes: www.enchantedlearning.com/Rhymes.html

Dr. Seuss. (1960). *One Fish, Two Fish, Red Fish, Blue Fish.* New York: Random House.

Dr. Seuss. (1957). *The Cat in the Hat.* New York: Random House.

PowerPoint Activity

1. Students open the *Rhyming Words* template in PowerPoint.

2. Students click on the text box to enter their name on the title slide. The words will appear where the cursor flashes. Students then move to the next slide by pressing the Page Down key on the keyboard.

3. Students read the verse and select a word that rhymes with another by clicking, holding down the mouse, and dragging it over the word to highlight it. Students then change the font color of the rhyming words.

    *   If students accidentally drag words or letters around while trying to highlight, they can use the Undo button on the Standard toolbar. This is also helpful if words or a whole slide are deleted.

- To change the color of a word students go the Drawing toolbar and click on the Font Color button.

4. Students insert pictures from the Clip Art Gallery to illustrate the rhymes and words on each slide. The pictures can be resized and moved.

   - To insert clip art, students go to the Drawing toolbar and click on the Insert Clip Art button. They enter a descriptive word for the picture they are looking for in the search box and press Search. Students then select a picture from the search results and insert it into the slide, either by double-clicking it, or by single-clicking it and then pressing Insert.

   - To resize the picture proportionally, students click on a corner handlebar and, holding down the mouse button, drag it diagonally to the desired size. To move the picture within the slide, students click and hold down the mouse button in the center of the picture and drag it to the desired location.

5. Students print the slides, six per page on a color printer if possible. To print, students go the File menu and click on Print > Print What > Handouts > 6 slides per page > OK. Students might need assistance printing handouts.

Extensions and Modifications

- Students copy a nursery rhyme of their choice from a book, highlight rhyming words, and illustrate with pictures to convey meaning. They may also insert slides and choose their own words to rhyme.

- Students can use the blank last slide of the *Rhyming Words* template to write their own rhyming lines of poetry (Fig. 19.3).

Hi
My name is Ty
I am sad
So give me my Dad

Figure 19.3 Sample verse written by a first grader.

PowerPoint Magic

Lesson 20 • Mother's Day Poem

Grades 4, 5

Lesson Description

In this lesson students write a Mother's Day poem or a poem for another special person. First, review relevant poem structure, formats, rhyming schemes, and samples with students. Students then compose their poem using the *Special Person Poem* template to guide their writing, help structure their poem, and keep the rhyme scheme regular. The outline for the poem, illustrated in Figure 20.1, is adapted from *Writing Poetry with Chidren*, an Evan-Moor resource for teachers.

Students writers focus on one stanza per PowerPoint slide, can easily move back and forth from main ideas to details, and always have an overview of the whole poem, which is visible in the Outline pane. To help with word choice, students can use an online rhyming dictionary such as RhymeZone.

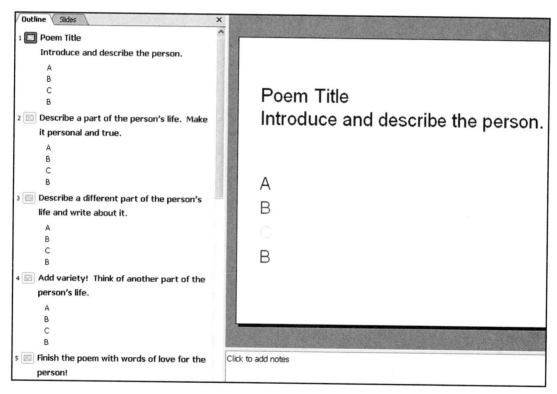

Figure 20.1 Students use the *Special Person Poem* template for writing a Mother's Day poem. As they work on each stanza in the Slide pane, the entire poem is visible in the Outline pane.

After completing all the stanzas, students send the poem to Microsoft Word (Fig. 20.2). Once in Microsoft Word, students remove all instructions and rhyme-scheme letters ("A-B-C-B") from the template. Students then choose a font and color to match the tone of the poem, and draw a picture in a drawing program and paste it at the bottom of the poem (Fig. 20.3). Depending on their experience, students may prefer to print the poem and illustrate with crayons or markers instead.

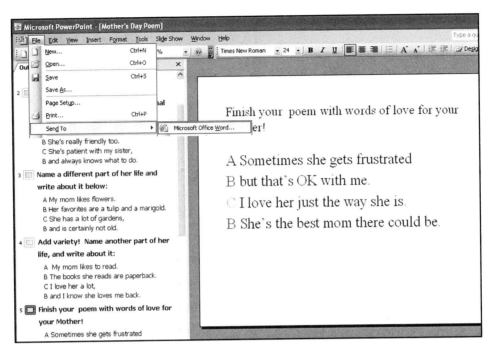

Figure 20.2 How to send a completed PowerPoint poem to Microsoft Word

Figure 20.3 A sample poem written and illustrated by a student

Assessment

Students use the *Mother's Day Poem* assessment to help guide them in this activity. Teachers use this assessment, which is provided on the CD as an Excel document that can be modified, to grade the assignment.

Higher Order Thinking Skills	Computer Skills Practiced	Subject Areas and Standards Addressed
Analysis: Students analyze why their mother (or grandmother) is important to them and explain this in a poem. Students organize their thoughts and share them in the given format. **Synthesis:** Students create and share an original poem using the given structure.	Insert and edit text in text boxes Move between Outline pane and Slide pane Use Page Down to move to the next slide Send a slide outline to Microsoft Word	NETS•S: 1.a, b; 2.b English Language Arts: NL-ENG.K-12.4, 5

Resources Needed

Online rhyming dictionary such as RhymeZone (www.rhymezone.com)

Rhyming dictionary such as Merriam-Webster's Rhyming Dictionary

Writing Poetry with Children, Grades 1–6, published by Evan-Moor (2008)

PowerPoint Activity

1. Students open the *Special Person Poem* template in PowerPoint.

2. Students click on the first slide in the Slide pane and double-click on a text box to change the words.

   • To move to the next slide, students click on a different slide in the Outline pane. Students click on the Slide pane to start making changes to the slide.

3. Students save the file when finished writing.

4. Students send the slide show to Microsoft Word. They go to the File menu and click on Send To > Microsoft Word, then choose Outline only in the dialogue box (Fig. 20.4).

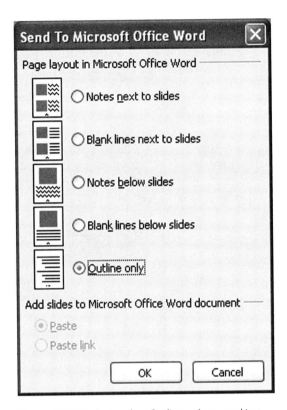

Figure 20.4 Students select Outline only to send just the words on the slide.

5. The document will open in Word. Students remove instructions and the rhyme-scheme letters (A-B-C-B). They can then enhance the poem by changing the font color and adding artwork.

Extensions and Modifications

Teachers can modify the template and have students write a poem on a different topic with a different number of stanzas with a different, assigned rhyme scheme.

Lesson 21 • Picturing Poetry

Grades 6–8

Lesson Description

Some students may find poetry less than engaging. This lesson introduces students to very accessible poems in the book *Doodle Dandies: Poems That Take Shape*. The poems in this book are illustrated; in fact, the words themselves form parts of the illustrations. Students are challenged to write and illustrate a poem in the same style, where the words become a part of the illustration. This allows students to work simultaneously on the visual and the verbal, inspiring both kinds of learners.

Review several poems from *Doodle Dandies: Poems That Take Shape* and other poetry books and Web sites, pointing out and discussing important elements of poetry such as rhyme, alliteration, personification, simile, metaphor, and onomatopoeia. In groups, have students pick out poems and identify various poetic elements. When looking at poems from *Doodle Dandies*, encourage students to note how the poems and the illustrations work together to create meaning.

Next, have students individually come up with a concept: an object, animal, or idea they would like to write a poem about. Whatever their concept, it should be something they feel they can draw a picture of fairly easily.

Finally, have students use PowerPoint to bring the visual and the verbal together. Using multiple text boxes, students jot down words and phrases that evoke their concept. Students should use at least two different elements of poetry. At the same time, students use PowerPoint's drawing tools and WordArt tool to illustrate their concept. Encourage students to switch back and forth between drawing and writing. As the illustration begins to take shape, have students start to fit the text boxes into the illustration. The shape and placement of the poem's words should echo or support the poem's illustration (Fig. 21.1).

Compile all student slides into a single slide show. As a class, view everyone's poetry, noting the various elements of poetry that are used and how the words fit into the illustration.

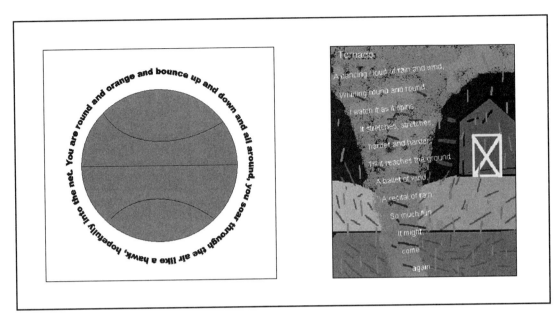

Figure 21.1 Poems become part of their illustrations, resulting in exciting works of art.

Alternatively, you can encourage students to give visual structure to their words. The result can, for example, be a shape poem, a diamante (a diamond-shaped poem of seven lines), or a cinquain poem (a five-line poem). This type of activity helps students to review verbs, adjectives, nouns, and gerunds in an interesting and creative way. If students need more structure, the Picturing Poetry template can be used to help students develop ideas for their poems and give them a form to express themselves.

Figure 21.2 shows the structure of a diamante poem along with a student example. Note how the text and drawing combined highlight the intended meaning of the poem. Font size and colors can be used to emphasize the contrast and comparisons.

1 noun,	**Man**
2 adjectives describing that noun,	**Rational, Kind**
3 verbs or gerunds done by that noun,	**Eating, Helping, Laughing**
2 nouns related to the first noun and 2 nouns related to its antonym,	**Skin, Fingers, Fur, Claws**
3 verbs or gerunds done by the antonym,	**Howling, Harming, Devouring**
2 adjectives describing the antonym,	**Ferocious, Wild**
1 noun that is the antonym of (or renames) the first noun.	**Werewolf**

Figure 21.2 Diamante poem structure and student example.

Students can, of course, also insert original drawings into these poems to help add voice and meaning.

Assessment

Students use the *Picturing Poetry* rubric to help guide them in writing and illustrating their poems. The rubric is provided on the accompanying CD as a Word document that can be modified by the teacher.

Higher Order Thinking Skills	Computer Skills Practiced	Subject Areas and Standards Addressed
Analysis: Arrange the words of a poem to support an illustration **Synthesis:** Write a poem and draw a picture; design the layout for visual impact	Use Draw tools Use basic shapes, fill with color; change line color Use scribble tool for free-hand drawing Insert and rotate a text box Insert and format WordArt Format text: alignment, font, color, size	NETS•S: 1.a, b; 2.b English Language Arts: NL-ENG.K-12.4, 6

Resources Needed

Doodle Dandies: Poems That Take Shape by J. Patrick Lewis, images by Lisa Desimimi (Scholastic, 2000)

Poetry books or Web sites to use as examples

PowerPoint Activity

1. Students open a new blank presentation in PowerPoint.

2. Students insert text boxes and type words and phrases that evoke their concept.

    - To insert a text box, students go to the Drawing toolbar and click on the Text Box icon. They then click on the spot where they want to place the text box.

3. Students use the drawing tools to illustrate their writing. Students click on the AutoShapes menu on the Drawing Toolbar, and then use the Lines and Basic Shapes (Fig. 21.3) to make a drawing.

- After selecting a tool, students drag on the slide to make a drawing. To make a perfect circle, square, or a perfectly straight line, they can hold down the Shift key on the keyboard as they draw. When the drawing is complete, students click on it to select it so that the handlebars are visible.

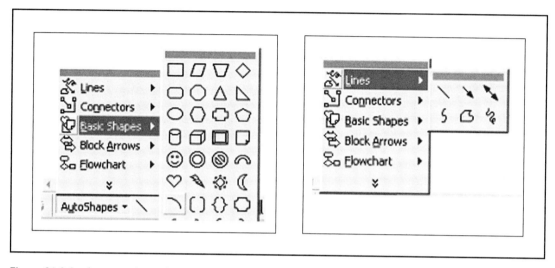

Figure 21.3 Students use the tools in Basic Shapes on the Draw menu, like the Oval and Arc shapes, as well as the Lines tool, to draw on a PowerPoint slide.

4. Students can click on the arrow next to the Fill Color button on the Drawing Toolbar, and select a color, or, click on More Fill Colors or Fill Effects for more choices. They can change the line color by clicking on the shape to select it, and then clicking on the arrow next to the Line Color button on the Drawing Toolbar. They can select a color, or click on More Line Colors or Patterned Lines for more options.

5. Students can format their text to add meaning or aid in fitting text into their illustration. To rotate a text box, students should click on the border of the text box, so that the handlebars are visible. Then they click on the Free Rotate button on the Drawing Toolbar; the text box will have a green dot in each corner. They grab one of the green dots and drag to rotate.

   - To insert WordArt, students click on the WordArt icon on the Drawing Toolbar, select the style of writing, click on OK, type in the text, and then click on OK to place it on the slide. They click on the WordArt to select it, drag to move it, and drag the handlebars to resize it. Or, they can click on the WordArt to select it, and click on the WordArt Shape button, (ABC), on the WordArt toolbar to change its shape. They may need to experiment with breaking a phrase into parts and inserting new WordArt piece by piece on the slide in order to get the exact effect they desire.

6. To save the slide show and print full page slides in color, students go to the File menu and click on Save; then click on Print > OK.

Extensions and Modifications

Students read a poem and illustrate it. Students as young as first grade can do this exercise. They can learn to distinguish between literal and figurative meanings of words, and reflect this in their drawings or choice of clip art. You can instruct students to convey the figurative meaning with their illustrations, for example. Each line of poetry can be placed on a new slide and saved as a template that students open to read and illustrate.

Figure 21.4 Students illustrate poems with clip art.

Visualization and Graphic Representation Lessons

Use Graphic Organizers

Lesson 22 • Greater Than, Less Than, or Equal To?

Grade 1

Lesson Description

Students create and solve math problems using "greater than" and "less than," first with pieces of candy, or similar objects, then with pictures of candy. They group the pictures to represent two numbers of their choice, type the numbers, and use the > and < signs to compare the numbers. This lesson helps students to connect abstract numbers and mathematical symbols with concrete objects and images to develop understanding of mathematical concepts.

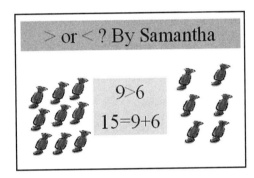

Figure 22.1 A student illustrates a math problem.

Model the problem by dividing the class into two groups. Show the class 15 actual pieces of candy. Split the candy between the two groups of students, giving one group 9 pieces and the other 6. Open up the *Greater Than Less Than* template, insert a picture of candy, and duplicate the picture 14 times to get 15 pictures. Group the pictures on each side of the slide to match the division of the actual candy between the groups, have students determine which group has more, and type 9>6 (Fig. 22.1).

Individually, students open the *Greater Than Less Than* template in PowerPoint and recreate this problem on the first slide.

To take the concepts further, ask if the two groups were happy with the way the candies were shared. Have students brainstorm a way to make the division fair. They determine that 7=7, and that one candy must be removed by the teacher. The teacher duplicates this solution on the next slide, entering 7=7, dividing the pictures of candy into two groups of 7, and then dragging one piece of candy away and labeling it "Teacher."

In the *Greater Than Less Than* template, students also recreate this problem. Now, have students go to the third slide. Give them two unequal numbers, and have them duplicate and group pictures of candy to match and use the < or > sign to complete the problem. On the fourth slide, have students figure out a way to fairly split the candy from the third slide, and have them illustrate the problem. If desired, repeat with a new problem on the fifth and sixth slides; otherwise, have students delete the fifth and sixth slides if they aren't used. You can also direct students to insert more slides if needed.

Assessment

Students use the *Greater Than Less Than* checklist to help guide them in this activity. The checklist is provided on the accompanying CD as an Excel document that can be modified by the teacher.

Higher Order Thinking Skills	Computer Skills Practiced	Subject Areas and Standards Addressed
Application: Solve the problem of sharing the candies fairly between two groups	Insert clip art	NETS•S: 1.a, b; 2.b; 4.b
	Duplicate clip art using Ctrl-D	Math: NM-NUM.PK-2.1; NM-ALG.PK-2.2, 3
Analysis: Connect abstract numbers and mathematical symbols with concrete objects and images to develop understanding of mathematical concepts	Move and resize clip art images	English Language Arts: NL-ENG.K-12.4, .5, .12
	Enter text, numbers, and the signs >, <, and =	
	Use the Page Down key to move to the next slide	
Synthesis: Create examples of math problems with greater than, less than, or equal to expressions	Insert new slides and delete unwanted slides from the template	
	Print slides	
Evaluation: Compare the number of objects in two groups, and divide the total into two equal halves		

Resources Needed

Pieces of candy or similar objects

PowerPoint Activity

1. Students open the *Greater Than Less Than* template in PowerPoint.

2. Students insert a piece of clip art into the slide and then resize it.

   • To insert clip art, students go to the Drawing toolbar and click on the Insert Clip Art button. They enter a descriptive word for the picture they are looking for in the search box and press Search. Students then select a picture from the search results and insert it into the slide, either by double-clicking it, or by single-clicking it and then pressing Insert.

- To resize the picture proportionally, students click on a corner handlebar and, holding down the mouse button, drag it diagonally to the desired size.

3. Students click on the picture to select it, hold down the Ctrl button on the keyboard, and press the D key to duplicate the picture. Students repeat this several times, duplicating the number of pictures needed for the activity.

4. Students move (click and drag) the pictures into two groups and count how many are in each group. They should click on the light blue text box to write the problem; for example: 9>6.

5. Students press the Page Down key to move to the next slide. Now have students drag the pictures into two equal groups. If there is a leftover image, they should drag it to a separate area. They should click on the light blue text box to write the problem, for example: 7=7.

6. Students press the Page Down key on the keyboard to move to the next slide and make a new greater than or less than problem using different pictures and numbers.

7. To delete a slide, students can click on it in the Outline pane and click on the Delete key; to insert a slide, students choose Insert, then New Slide.

8. Students print the slides, six per page. To print the slides, students go to the File menu and click Print > Print What > Handouts > 6 slides per page > OK. Students may need supervision to print correctly.

Extensions and Modifications

The teacher can choose clip art to reflect holidays or special events; for example, ghosts in October or Valentine's Day candy in February.

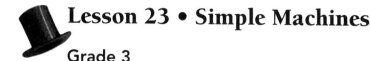

Lesson 23 • Simple Machines

Grade 3

Lesson Description

Students often need to visualize new concepts. In this lesson, students are introduced to the concept of simple machines. This lesson was developed with third-grade teacher Carole DeYoung, who found that students retain the material better after participating in this straightforward PowerPoint exercise.

Students gather information from textbooks or grade-appropriate Web sites that offer information about and photographs of simple machines such as a wheel and axle, lever, screw, inclined plane, gears, and pulley. They create a booklet that defines and illustrates each type of machine they encounter, making slides with clip art or photographs of real machines copied from the Web. They identify what the machine is used for and give an example of how they might use each machine in their daily lives (Fig. 23.1).

1. lever

• A lever is a board that helps you move objects easily. I use a seesaw to lift my friend's weight.

Figure 23.1 Student example of a simple machine

The *Simple Machines* template provides a slide for each of the simple machines. Students can name the machine in the title. In the text box, they explain what each machine does, how they use it, and give an example that they use. Finally, they add an appropriate graphic for each. A list of previewed online resources is given on the last slide; in Slide Show view students can click the links to open them in a browser window. Students print the slide show as a booklet and can use it to review for a quiz on simple machines.

Assessment

Students complete the *Simple Machines* checklist to help them monitor their completion of the task. The checklist is provided on the accompanying CD as an Excel document that can be modified by the teacher.

Higher Order Thinking Skills	Computer Skills Practiced	Subject Areas and Standards Addressed
Analysis: Students read, analyze, and apply their understanding of machines in order to write a brief outline or definition of each machine. **Synthesis:** Students create an original booklet to explain simple machines. **Evaluation:** Students connect the concepts with visual cues to help remember and understand.	Insert text on a slide Save a slide show Click a hyperlink to open it Navigate on a Web page, click on hyperlinks, and use the back button Use the taskbar to move between a PowerPoint document and a Web browser Copy a picture from a Web page and paste it into a PowerPoint document	NETS•S: 1.a, b; 2.b; 3.a, b, c Science: NS.K-4.2 Physical Science English Language Arts: NL-ENG.K-12.1

Resources Needed

Edheads Activities—Simple Machines worksheet for students, helps identify and define simple machines:
http://edheads.org/activities/simple-machines/simple-machines-pre-test.pdf

How Stuff Works, for students who want to explore a specific machine and add interesting details: www.howstuffworks.com

Inquiry Almanac Spotlight on Simple Machines: www.fi.edu/qa97/spotlight3/

Mikids Simple Machines, for basic definitions and photographs: www.mikids.com/Smachines.htm

PowerPoint Activity

1. Students open the *Simple Machines* template in PowerPoint

2. Students click on the text box on Slide 1 to enter their names.

3. Students enter the names of the seven simple machines in the Outline pane (Fig. 23.2).

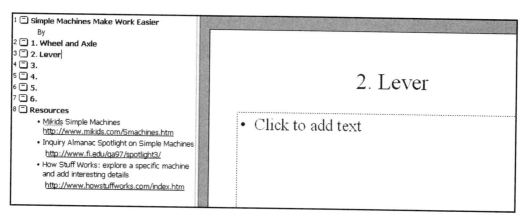

Figure 23.2 Students click on the Outline pane and enter the names of the simple machines.

4. Students click on each slide and define the simple machine, entering text in the appropriate text box. They should use their own words.

5. Students use the links on the Resources page to find and insert photographs. Teachers should discuss with students the basic rules of copyright law and how to give credit. In Slide Show view, students can simply click one of the hyperlinks on the last slide to launch the chosen Web site in their browser. To open the Web site from Outline view, they right-click on the Web address, move the mouse over Hyperlink, and click on Open (Fig. 23.3).

Students can move between the PowerPoint document and the Web page by clicking on the name of the document in the Taskbar.

• To copy a picture from a Web site, students right-click on the picture, then left-click on Copy. They return to the PowerPoint slide, right-click on the slide, then click on Paste.

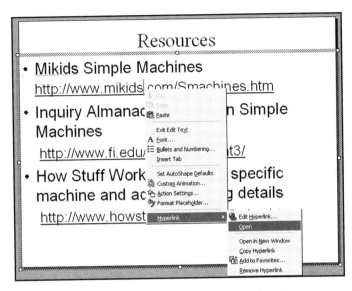

Figure 23.3 In Outline view, students right-click a Web address, move the mouse over Hyperlink, then click on Open to launch that Web page in a browser window.

6. Students save and print their completed assignment. To print the slides, students go to the File menu and click on Print > Print What > Handouts > 6 slides per page > OK. Students cut out the pages and staple them together.

Extensions and Modifications

- Students who complete the assignment quickly could go to the How Things Work Web page to get details and interesting information about one or more of the samples of simple machines they have already identified. They might search for information on a bicycle or a tower crane, for example.

- Students with advanced computer skills can draw a representation of each simple machine on the slide using the Basic Shapes, and Line tools on the Drawing toolbar. Other students can draw this with a pencil on the hard copy after it is printed.

- The teacher can provide materials to students for making something that looks like or works like a simple machine.

References and Resources

Assessment by rubrics or portfolios

Rubistar: http://rubistar.4teachers.org

Big6 research technique

The Big6 homepage: www.big6.com

Bloom's taxonomy

Bloom, B. S. (1984) *Taxonomy of educational objectives.* Boston, MA: Allyn & Bacon.

University of Victoria—Learning Skills: www.coun.uvic.ca/learning/exams/blooms-taxonomy.html

Brain-based learning

Gardner, H. (1993). *Multiple intelligences: The theory in practice.* New York: Basic Books.

Gardner. H. (2000) *Intelligence reframed: Multiple intelligences for the 21st century,* New York: Basic Books.

Differentiated instruction

Gregory, G. H. & Chapman, C. (2006). *Differentiated instructional strategies: One size doesn't fit all* (2nd ed.). Thousand Oaks, CA: Corwin Press.

Robert J. Marzano, R. J., Pickering, D., Pollock, J. E. (2004). *Classroom instruction that works: Research-based strategies for increasing student achievement.* Upper Saddle River, NJ: Prentice Hall.

Tomlinson, C. A. (2003). *Fulfilling the promise of the differentiated classroom: Strategies and tools for responsive teaching.* Alexandria, VA: ASCD

KWHL charts

Midlink Magazine's KWHL chart: www.ncsu.edu/midlink/KWL.chart.html

Multimedia learning theory/dual coding/cognitive load

Mayer, R. E. (2001). *Multimedia learning.* New York: Cambridge University Press.

Mayer, R. E., Heiser, J., Lonn, S. (2001, March) Cognitive constraints on multimedia learning: When presenting more material results in less understanding. *Journal of Educational Psychology* 93(1) pp.187–198.

PowerPointlessness?

Hlynka, D., Mason, R. (1998, Sept-Oct) PowerPoint in the classroom: What is the point? *Educational Technology Journal* 38(5), pp. 42–45.

Keller, J. (2003, January). Is PowerPoint the devil? *Chicago Tribune*. Available at http://faculty.winthrop.edu/kosterj/WRIT465/management/juliakeller1.htm

Tufte, E. (2003, September) PowerPoint is evil: Power corrupts. PowerPoint corrupts absolutely. *Wired Magazine*. Available at www.wired.com/wired/archive/11.09/ppt2.html

McKenzie, J. (2000). Scoring power points. *From Now On 10*(1) n.p. Available at www.fno.org/sept00/powerpoints.html

Project based learning

4Teachers.org's Project Based Learning: Checklists to support Project Based Learning and evaluation: http://pblchecklist.4teachers.org

6 + 1 Trait writing

Northwest Regional Educational Laboratory: www.nwrel.org/assessment/department.php?d=1

6 + 1 Trait Writing: Scoring Continuum: www.nwrel.org/assessment/pdfRubrics/6plus1traits.PDF#search=%22Writing%20Styles%20six%20traits%22

Using PowerPoint effectively

Atkinson, C. (2005). *Beyond bullet points: Using Microsoft PowerPoint to create presentations that inform, motivate, and inspire*. Redmond, WA: Microsoft Press.

Visual learning

Institute for the Advancement of Research in Education. (2003, July). *Graphic organizers: A review of scientifically based research*. Available from www.inspiration.com/vlearning/research/

Writing with computers

Purdue University Online Writing Lab: Writing with Computers: http://owl.english.purdue.edu/handouts/general/gl_computer.html

Kodak's Top 10 Tips for Great Pictures: www.kodak.com/eknec/PageQuerier.jhtml?pq-path=38/39/317&pq-locale=en_US

Web English Teacher, Writing Resources: www.webenglishteacher.com/writing.html

Son of Citation Machine, Web site for generating MLA or APA style references: www.citationmachine.net

Writing styles

Purdue University Online Writing Lab: PowerPoint Presentations: http://owl.english.purdue.edu/workshops/pp/

KidsKonnect.com: Writing Styles: www.kidskonnect.com/content/view/350/27/

Appendix A

Basic Instructions for PowerPoint 2007

The Ribbon

The 2007 version of PowerPoint replaces menus and toolbars with the Ribbon. The top row of the Ribbon shows the main tabs, which are always visible. The main tabs include Home, Insert, Design, Animations, Slide Show, Review, View, and Format. When you click on a main tab on the Ribbon, you will then see the groups and command buttons. For example, the Home tab includes the Slides group, which includes the New Slide, Layout, Reset, and Delete command buttons. The Using Main Tabs, Groups, and Command Buttons section of this appendix provides an in-depth listing of how to find and use the command buttons.

A contextual tab will also become active if you click on an object such as a picture, shape, or table. For example, if you click on WordArt to modify it, the Drawing Tools contextual tab will appear and provide you with the relevant command buttons.

Remember, just as in previous versions of PowerPoint, always select the item you want to change, then click on the button to change it. An easy way to find a command is to right-click on the text or object you want to change and select from the menu that appears.

Other Commands

Office button: Click on the Office button to locate the commands formerly found under the File menu, such as Save, Save As, Print, Page Setup, and Send to Word.

Quick Access bar: Click on the Quick Access bar to Undo, Redo, and Save. You can modify the bar to add Print.

Slide view: Click on the buttons on the bottom right corner of the window to change the view.

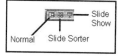

Keyboard shortcuts: All keyboard shortcuts for previous versions of PowerPoint also work in PowerPoint 2007.

Using Main Tabs, Groups, and Command Buttons

Home Tab

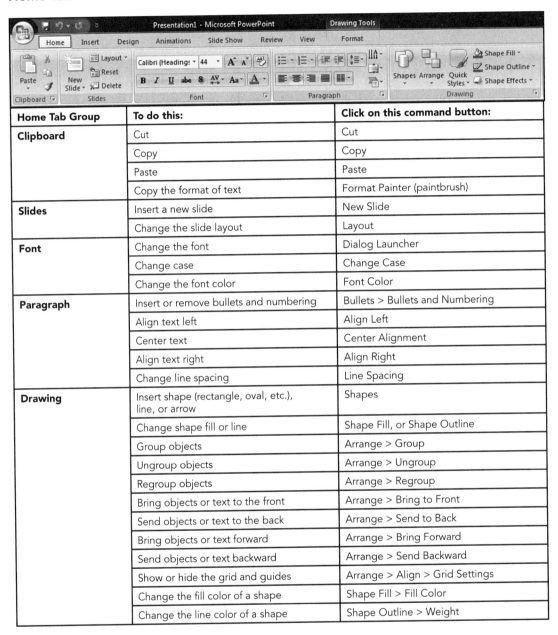

Home Tab Group	To do this:	Click on this command button:
Clipboard	Cut	Cut
	Copy	Copy
	Paste	Paste
	Copy the format of text	Format Painter (paintbrush)
Slides	Insert a new slide	New Slide
	Change the slide layout	Layout
Font	Change the font	Dialog Launcher
	Change case	Change Case
	Change the font color	Font Color
Paragraph	Insert or remove bullets and numbering	Bullets > Bullets and Numbering
	Align text left	Align Left
	Center text	Center Alignment
	Align text right	Align Right
	Change line spacing	Line Spacing
Drawing	Insert shape (rectangle, oval, etc.), line, or arrow	Shapes
	Change shape fill or line	Shape Fill, or Shape Outline
	Group objects	Arrange > Group
	Ungroup objects	Arrange > Ungroup
	Regroup objects	Arrange > Regroup
	Bring objects or text to the front	Arrange > Bring to Front
	Send objects or text to the back	Arrange > Send to Back
	Bring objects or text forward	Arrange > Bring Forward
	Send objects or text backward	Arrange > Send Backward
	Show or hide the grid and guides	Arrange > Align > Grid Settings
	Change the fill color of a shape	Shape Fill > Fill Color
	Change the line color of a shape	Shape Outline > Weight

Insert Tab

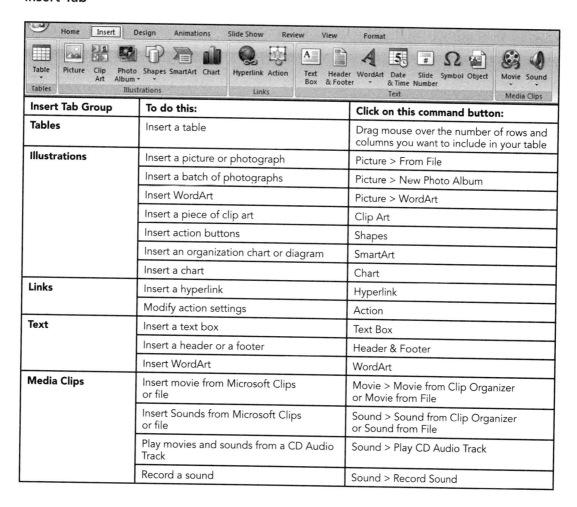

Insert Tab Group	To do this:	Click on this command button:
Tables	Insert a table	Drag mouse over the number of rows and columns you want to include in your table
Illustrations	Insert a picture or photograph	Picture > From File
	Insert a batch of photographs	Picture > New Photo Album
	Insert WordArt	Picture > WordArt
	Insert a piece of clip art	Clip Art
	Insert action buttons	Shapes
	Insert an organization chart or diagram	SmartArt
	Insert a chart	Chart
Links	Insert a hyperlink	Hyperlink
	Modify action settings	Action
Text	Insert a text box	Text Box
	Insert a header or a footer	Header & Footer
	Insert WordArt	WordArt
Media Clips	Insert movie from Microsoft Clips or file	Movie > Movie from Clip Organizer or Movie from File
	Insert Sounds from Microsoft Clips or file	Sound > Sound from Clip Organizer or Sound from File
	Play movies and sounds from a CD Audio Track	Sound > Play CD Audio Track
	Record a sound	Sound > Record Sound

Design Tab

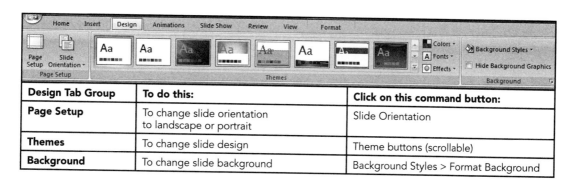

Design Tab Group	To do this:	Click on this command button:
Page Setup	To change slide orientation to landscape or portrait	Slide Orientation
Themes	To change slide design	Theme buttons (scrollable)
Background	To change slide background	Background Styles > Format Background

Animations Tab

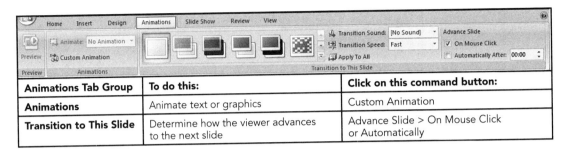

Animations Tab Group	To do this:	Click on this command button:
Animations	Animate text or graphics	Custom Animation
Transition to This Slide	Determine how the viewer advances to the next slide	Advance Slide > On Mouse Click or Automatically

Review Tab

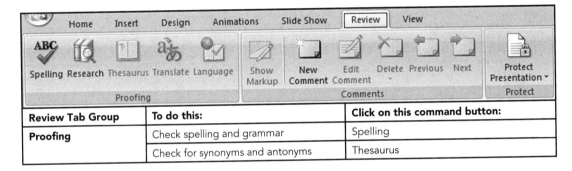

Review Tab Group	To do this:	Click on this command button:
Proofing	Check spelling and grammar	Spelling
	Check for synonyms and antonyms	Thesaurus

Format Tab

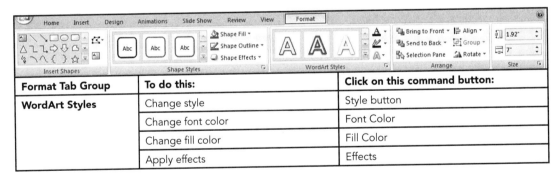

Format Tab Group	To do this:	Click on this command button:
WordArt Styles	Change style	Style button
	Change font color	Font Color
	Change fill color	Fill Color
	Apply effects	Effects

Format Tab—Contextual Picture Tools

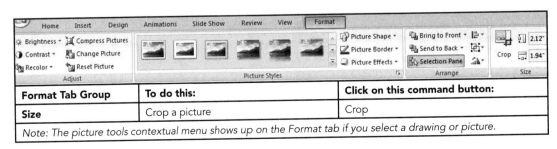

Format Tab Group	To do this:	Click on this command button:
Size	Crop a picture	Crop
Note: The picture tools contextual menu shows up on the Format tab if you select a drawing or picture.		

Appendix B

Scope and Sequence Chart of Internet Research Skills

The ability to use the Internet effectively is a crucial skill for students to have and many of the lessons in this book require students to do research online. Therefore, it is important for educators to define the Internet research skills that students need to master in order to monitor and promote them. The following scope and sequence chart helps to define those skills. Notice that students' skills develop gradually, from using preselected resources in the early elementary grades to performing complex searches and being aware of digital citizenship issues in upper elementary and middle school grades.

Behavioral outcome	Specific skills mastered	Grade				
		1	2	3	4	5–8
Navigate the Internet	Open web browser	X	X	X	X	X
	Use Forward, Back, and Close buttons	X	X	X	X	X
	Identify hyperlinked text	X	X	X	X	X
	Refresh a Web page	X	X	X	X	X
	Read a Web page and find information		X	X	X	X
	Use the View menu to go to a site, Use Favorites to bookmark a site			X	X	X
Copy pictures from the Internet and paste into PowerPoint	Use Microsoft Office Online Clip Art		X	X	X	X
Copy text from the Internet and paste into PowerPoint	Highlight text then copy and paste		X	X	X	X
Acknowledge sources	Use the taskbar or Alt-Tab to switch between applications. Paste in the web address of sources		X	X	X	X
	Use Son of Citation Machine for MLA/APA format					X
Search the Internet for good resources	Use a student-friendly search engine			X	X	X
	Select a search engine, use advanced search strategies					X
Write text with hyperlinks						X
Save a PowerPoint slide show or Word document as a Web page						X
Attitudes and Understanding						
Understand how the Internet works	Understand the terms Internet, network, intranet, extranet, service provider, browser					X
	Learn basic HTML					X
Understand legal and ethical responsibilities, netiquette	Use CyberSmart online resources at www.cybersmartcurriculum. org/curr_over/					X
Be aware of internet safety issues	Maintain privacy of information while e-mailing and chatting					X
Be aware of inaccuracies and biases found on some Internet sites	Evaluate web sites. Identify primary and secondary sources					X

Appendix C

National Educational Technology Standards for Students (NETS•S)

The National Educational Technology Standards for students are divided into six broad categories. Standards within each category are to be introduced, reinforced, and mastered by students. Teachers can use these standards as guidelines for planning technology-based activities in which students achieve success in learning, communication, and life skills.

1. **Creativity and Innovation**

   Students demonstrate creative thinking, construct knowledge, and develop innovative products and processes using technology. Students:

   a. apply existing knowledge to generate new ideas, products, or processes.

   b. create original works as a means of personal or group expression.

   c. use models and simulations to explore complex systems and issues.

   d. identify trends and forecast possibilities.

2. **Communication and Collaboration**

   Students use digital media and environments to communicate and work collaboratively, including at a distance, to support individual learning and contribute to the learning of others. Students:

   a. interact, collaborate, and publish with peers, experts, or others employing a variety of digital environments and media.

   b. communicate information and ideas effectively to multiple audiences using a variety of media and formats.

   c. develop cultural understanding and global awareness by engaging with learners of other cultures.

   d. contribute to project teams to produce original works or solve problems.

3. **Research and Information Fluency**

   Students apply digital tools to gather, evaluate, and use information. Students:

   a. plan strategies to guide inquiry.

   b. locate, organize, analyze, evaluate, synthesize, and ethically use information from a variety of sources and media.

c. evaluate and select information sources and digital tools based on the appropriateness to specific tasks.

d. process data and report results.

4. **Critical Thinking, Problem Solving, and Decision Making**

Students use critical-thinking skills to plan and conduct research, manage projects, solve problems, and make informed decisions using appropriate digital tools and resources. Students:

a. identify and define authentic problems and significant questions for investigation.

b. plan and manage activities to develop a solution or complete a project.

c. collect and analyze data to identify solutions and make informed decisions.

d. use multiple processes and diverse perspectives to explore alternative solutions.

5. **Digital Citizenship**

Students understand human, cultural, and societal issues related to technology and practice legal and ethical behavior. Students:

a. advocate and practice the safe, legal, and responsible use of information and technology.

b. exhibit a positive attitude toward using technology that supports collaboration, learning, and productivity.

c. demonstrate personal responsibility for lifelong learning.

d. exhibit leadership for digital citizenship.

6. **Technology Operations and Concepts**

Students demonstrate a sound understanding of technology concepts, systems, and operations. Students:

a. understand and use technology systems.

b. select and use applications effectively and productively.

c. troubleshoot systems and applications.

d. transfer current knowledge to the learning of new technologies.